Carol Young has never seen herself as anything other than an ordinary person. From an unassuming suburban childhood to training as a stylist in a prestigious salon—and eventually owning her own salons, not only in her hometown of Edinburgh but also in the Shetland Isles—her path seemed straightforward.

After marrying and moving, children in tow, she found herself uprooted and became an island girl—a fish out of water! All the while, she quietly wondered about her own backstory. Occasional revelations along the way sparked questions that remained unanswered.

It wasn't until retirement that her quest for the truth truly began, bringing with it the realization that her life had been much, much more than just ordinary.

Carol Young

I Wish I'd Asked More Questions

AUSTIN MACAULEY PUBLISHERS®

LONDON · CAMBRIDGE · NEW YORK · SHARJAH

Copyright © Carol Young 2025

The right of Carol Young to be identified as author of this work has been asserted by the author in accordance with sections 77 and 78 of the Copyright, Designs and Patents Act 1988.

All rights reserved. No part of this publication may be reproduced, stored in a retrieval system, or transmitted in any form or by any means, electronic, mechanical, photocopying, recording, or otherwise, without the prior permission of the publishers.

Any person who commits any unauthorised act in relation to this publication may be liable to criminal prosecution and civil claims for damages.

All of the events in this memoir are true to the best of author's memory. The views expressed in this memoir are solely those of the author.

A CIP catalogue record for this title is available from the British Library.

ISBN 9781035883172 (Paperback)
ISBN 9781035883189 (ePub e-book)

www.austinmacauley.com

First Published 2025
Austin Macauley Publishers Ltd®
1 Canada Square
Canary Wharf
London
E14 5AA

Introduction

This little story of my life was something I never, ever, thought possible. Being labelled 'slow' at school because I had difficulty with spelling, it would be many years before I would learn that I was, in fact, dyslexic. A revelation, it was, hearing of the plight of others such as Sir Jackie Stewart, on TV documentaries. Their word 'blindness' was just what I had always known. My occupation, dealing with so many disparate characters, was a life-long education in itself. One professional in a top job said never to worry; she would sketch out her words, then check and correct them with a dictionary later.

So, like many a celebrity!, I was forced to employ a ghostwriter. I didn't have to look far! Many aspects of my early years demanded answers, but to be seen and not heard was the norm. Only in later years have many of my questions been answered. Throughout my many years of hairdressing, I always tried my best for my clients, and I can say, hand on heart, that dissatisfied customers immediately got their money back. I remember them all, and I can count them on one hand.

Chapter 1

Mum, Cathy Farquhar Cirea-1952 (Photo: Author's collection)

The subject of our story, Carol, was born on 18 October 1949. Her place of birth was the Salvation Army Florence Booth House, in the Lochee district of Dundee. Clement Park was a refuge for young girls and ladies in distress, and for some a place of confinement prior to giving birth. The reasons for this particular circumstance make for quite a tale in itself, though we can be sure it was just so for many other inmates.

Carol's mother, Cathie, was a Mackenzie from Inverness, daughter of an Insurance salesman, well known in the area. The year 1919. A twin in a family of five, the youngest (just!), but soon to lose their mother. Fred, their father quickly remarried an older woman, who, having her own brood, did not take too well to adding another five. Little family history has trickled down to the present, other than that when Cathie left school, most probably at 14 years of age, she went into domestic service. Anecdotal evidence points to her spending quite a few years in the grand house of the Mackintosh family of raincoat fame.

As for so many, the Second World War changed everything, with the call-up for military service. Cathie joined the Royal Navy on 18 July 1940, and as a Wren cooked many a meal for shore-based Matelots. Latterly, she was based at the station at Hatston, near Kirkwall, Orkney. Cathie was de-mobbed come 20 March 1946. Her base captain held her to be hard working and reliable and signed her off as being of good character.

Nothing is known of her future until she appeared on the books of the City of Edinburgh's social services department. It then became apparent just what happened during the intervening years. Post-war, a female, even a fully trained cook might only find domestic employment. It would appear that Cathie had made for the city, finding work in such a capacity at the Nurse's Home in Chalmers Street, off Lauriston Place. Close by the Royal Dancing was still the major recreation back then for adults, and so it was that Cathie embarked on a ballroom romance. Swept off her feet, as it were, while dancing in one of Edinburgh's many dance halls. Records tell us that the affair was doomed. For her handsome beau, it was indeed an affair, as when Cathie announced that out of their love, a child was on the way, he quickly removed himself from her company. Yes, he was a married man.

To keep a child out of wedlock was almost unheard of; most such babies were given up for adoption, sometimes even before the birth. Also, back then, a single pregnant mother would usually seek another locality for her confinement, but also for the shame. So then, this is the circumstance of Carol's arrival in the land of the living. It became apparent that such was the bond between mother and baby, no adoption or removal of child from parent was on Cathie's agenda!

Adoption did, however, eventually become a near reality. Papers for this purpose were drawn up. Carol's new parents would be her Aunt Justine and Uncle Capt Noel Bowers. But, at the eleventh hour, Cathie rescinded the agreement. One can only wonder what stress and torment she was experiencing during this time, but there is no doubting her determination and love for her firstborn child.

Trying to find domestic work with a child in tow proved difficult, as one can imagine. At one point, with Carol being cared for by her prospective adoptive relatives, Cathie returned to the Citadel in Lochee and declared her intention to retain parenthood. In May of 1950, mother and child took the train to Edinburgh. Cathie then threw herself, and her circumstance, upon the mercy of the social services.

After one night in a Hostel at 5 The Vennel, both were placed in temporary accommodation at Glenlockhart, only recently cleared of quarantine restrictions. Within two months, Cathie was back at Lauriston, her wage £2.15/- per week. Now Carol was placed at St Katherine's Children's Home, Liberton.

Looking back, we can only imagine the heartache Aunt Justine suffered. Having the baby almost from birth, a sister for Joan, her only child. To give Carol back after many months left her desolate, such that she purchased a cinema ticket, then cried and cried in the darkened auditorium. This agony was compounded by the fact that she could have no more children.

Chapter 2

Mum visits at St. Katherines-1950 (Photo: Author's collection)

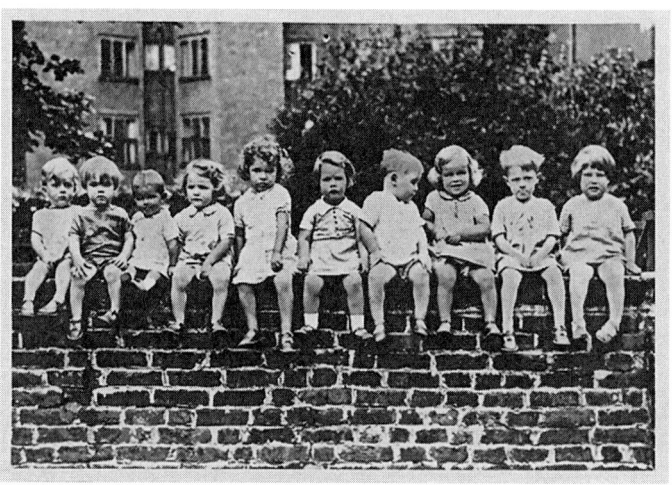

Fifth from right, Carol Young (Photo: Author's collection)

St Katherines was a red brick mansion-style house of some architectural significance, and at the time of my stay, was being run by Edinburgh City Council as a children's home. Whatever its history and appearance; it is no longer replaced by a scheme of private homes. Nearby, today, there exists a modern up-to-date facility still relating to children, but those of special needs. Records regarding my stay, sourced much later through Freedom of Information, reveal events between 25 July 1950 and 7 June 1952, not without problems, both medical and behavioural, it would appear. Most of my physical problems were simply that of any infant, but it makes for sobering reading the, non-medical, comments of some nurses.

The only worrying illness and I wonder how that came about, was having a stay in the City Hospital suffering from dysentery. On another occasion, apparently, I was examined by a doctor after a fall, I assume when released from my cot for exercise. Apart from a grazed forehead, arm movement caused tears, but X-rays cleared me of any injury soon mending. In one particular report, a post-script to my medical condition, a nurse had the temerity to append that I was 'not an attractive child, but personality improving!'

All through this time, my mother, though in full-time employment, was not having it at all easy. On meagre wages as a Scullery maid, with child care fees and accommodation to pay for, not a lot was left over for the odd dress or whatever I might require, what time off occasioned her irregular visits to St Katherine's. Of her evenings, I assume the generational pursuits of cinema and dancing fulfilled any recreation. Hence the courtship and subsequent marriage to my stepdad Jimmie Farquhar, prior to my release from care. Both were excellent dancers.

Much later, I learned that my broken-hearted Aunt Justine and Uncle Noel would pay me a visit when they could, bearing gifts. It seems much of my dress wear came from them. On release to the care of Mum and her new husband, medical notes state: plump, speaks fairly well, runs about, req. 3/16 inch raise inner side heels of shoes, to correct tendency for Knock-knees, possibly due to weight.

Release day arrived concurrent with the newlyweds securing rented accommodation in a small flat in Marchmont, Moncrieff Terrace. Soon, the City of Edinburgh would offer them the tenancy of a prefab in Duddingston, near Portobello.

Incidental to this chapter are the children in the dyke picture. At one time widely available in card shops, they were quite quickly identified as St Katherine inmates. Aunt Justine was immediate in her recognition, even after the passing years, averring that 'the dress you're wearing, we bought, and it was blue!' By the way, that's me mid-group, glowering.

Chapter 3

At the behest of WW2, Prime Minister Winston Churchill, in 1944, and looking to the future, a new style of home was designed. This was to meet the expected demand post-war… the prefab. What with the destruction meted out by the German Bombers on the UK, it wasn't only sites of industry targeted, but our very homes that were being flattened. On the site of the former military Duddingston Camp, redundant Nissen huts were pressed into service as makeshift accommodations for families. As these huts were dismantled, the new Prefabs were erected. In excess of 4,000 were built all over Edinburgh. In just such a building, the little Farquhar family took up residence.

Still, of course, an infant, my recall of this time is a bit sketchy. I do, however, remember fondly drifting off to sleep on an evening, with Scottish Dance music playing. This was after the Scottish news on the BBC Home Service. Also, Dad Jimmie would occasionally play along on the mouth organ, accompanying the many such bands of the time.

Mum reminded me years later of why I was such a tidy person. As a toddler, I was fascinated by a patch of mud at the bottom of our plot. Making mudpies came easy and was really quite enjoyable. Not, however, enjoyed by Mum was the state of my clothing after my sitting in the sun-warmed mud! I was instructed to take care of my clothes and not to dirty them in such a fashion again. The next day, I was straight back to my favourite place! Later, wondering just what could be capturing my attention, she came looking. My clothes she found clean, folded (after a fashion) in a small pile. Their owner sitting again in the mud, pies made, with mud smeared over much of her person!

My first experience of dog ownership was my dad's during this time. I doubt that any monies were involved in its procurement, most likely some stray. A loveable mongrel called Blanty(?), with a rough coat, mottled tan and white. It (I can't recall its gender) was affectionate to us all, and looked forward to long evening walks with his master, Jimmie. Protective of home territory, the fenced plot, the locals and their children were all told to leave well alone. Unfortunately, one young neighbour decided she knew better, reaching in over the gate, only to receive a bite.

A resultant sadness then at our address, as Blanty was immediately apprehended by the Constabulary, never to be seen again by anybody. That's just how it was back then.

My schooling began at Duddingston, not that I can remember much about it. What I do recall is that a neighbour, my school chum, decided that we should short-cut to and from school by way of a disused railway line. All was well until one day a man accosted us with offers of sweeties. Whether his appearance or demeanour was unsettling, we took off, running home without stopping. On arrival, I breathlessly informed Mum of this event to be given the age-old advice, 'Never take sweets from strangers.' Needless to say, it was a long way to our education thereafter.

In a prefab, which to this day is still held in high regard in certain quarters, the range is both the source of heating and for all cooking. Coal-fired, it was, along with the wireless (radio), the centre of the home. An occasion I do most memorably recall involved our stove. Mum informed me that I was, despite exhortations, jumping up and down on an easy chair, close by the range, whereby I fell but against the hot cast iron. Cold water application did not hide any tears. My burn was such that, after a hospital visit, I required much ointment and bandaging. Subsequent dressing removal and salve application were occasions I came to dread. Many years later, my husband enquired just why I, in my sleep, scratched something that was not there. It would appear that having scratched my extended arm, it would then fall across his sleeping face!

However pleasant, or otherwise, that life was at Duddingston, prefab living became undesirable with additions to our family, namely Shirley, then Linda, my new sisters. A move to more spacious quarters from our, now cramped, situation would be most welcome.

Chapter 4

Calders prefabs (Photo: Author's collection)

*Oxgangs Farm Gardens, Carol, left back and Shirley, left front
(Photo: Author's collection)*

The move to a flat in the new council scheme at Oxgangs, in the Colinton area of Edinburgh, was indeed most welcome. Duddingston's prefab had become exceedingly cramped as the family expanded. Any feeling of space soon disappeared with the arrival of my little brothers, Ian then Keith. Mum was never very well with her confinements and subsequent births. Despite exhortations from the family doctor, there appeared no stopping my uncompromising Dad.

Only when advised that, after Keith, she might not survive yet another birth, did he at last take heed. Around these difficult events, us girls were placed in homes, temporarily, usually for two weeks. With Ian's birth, I was to stay in the countryside at Humbie Home. Yet another experience—carbolic bath scrubbing, nit combed, a dose of syrup figs, then bedded after teatime. On Sundays, we were all marched, my fellow inmates and I, to the local church for worship and prayers. With Keith's birth, I was sent to stay with my Auntie Chrissie, Dad's sister. They stayed close by but in the private houses off Redford Road.

One night, there I saw a huge spider on the wall before lights-out. I pointed it out to my Cousin Marilyn, who let out a piercing scream. Her mum charged into the bedroom, and assuming I was the cause, proceeded to belabour my legs with a hairbrush! Her temperament was a match to that of her brother's. Once, while consoling me after a beating, Mum dropped a bombshell saying, "Anyway, he's not your real father." How could this be? I had surmised that it was because I, Carol Farquhar, being the eldest of his children, was used as an example to the others.

I can only remember my mum losing her temper with me once for giving her 'some lip'. She grabbed the kitchen broom and chased me from the living room. The bathroom door was locked, so I made for the main door, only to find she was in hot pursuit! Down the common stair, we shot, through the garden and into the street. Round the block we went, her threats ringing in my ears. Thankfully, she eventually gave up. With only two stations on TV at that time, a little light entertainment was provided that evening by Mum and myself. I remained outdoors for two to three hours before returning home, hoping all was calm – it was. Phew!

Being outdoors played a hugely enjoyable part in my pre-teen and early teen years. Squeezed between the posh houses past Caiystane up to Fairmilehead, and the Dreghorn Barracks was a wildlife wonderland. Many hours I spent with others, exploring the burns, streams and wooded copses in the valley leading up to Swanston village and farm. Today, it is a Motorway the City Bypass. The Hunter's Tryst was a Piggery and I was fascinated, leaning in over the dyke to watch them, more especially their piglets.

Interestingly, us kids had free rein in the Barracks, that is until much later after the IRA mainland bombings began. We all found it fascinating at festival times when rehearsals for the Tattoo took place. We especially loved the Gurkha soldiers who were so friendly and marched like a speeded-up film! Once I cut myself on some barbed wire and a kindly Nepalese, from his cigarette packet, separated the silver paper from its backing paper. This white paper he placed on my wound, so stemming the flow of blood. They also presented us with combs, brooches, trinket boxes and the like. All handmade, probably periods of boredom while stood down giving themselves something to do.

A near neighbour was wont to head up the burn past the covenanter monument. His purpose was to catch trout, if lucky. On occasion, some of us locals might benefit from a grilled trout for supper. Such a difference from the school dinner fish, swimming in a thick, gooey white sauce, flecked with a few spots of parsley!

Forever the Tomboy, I was just one of a gang forever wandering and exploring. My best 'mate' was Dave Mac from next door, who latterly would invite me to his room to listen to his record collection. His introduction to the likes of The Rolling Stones and The Pretty Things left this Monkees fan unimpressed! Our musical trysts never ventured beyond listening; he was just my pal.

Christmas times needless to say, were rather bleak in regard to presents. Santa's filling of all our stockings, left hanging by the mantelpiece might consist of a few shillings, a selection box, a jigsaw, maybe a pencil case. The only real toy I remember was a kiddie sewing machine, which I did appreciate. The cash, along with my earnings as a paper girl, went towards the purchase of scraps. These were treasured and placed lovingly in my scrapbook of which I was immensely proud.

A measure of just how tight money was, we had to endure freezing cold bedrooms. Overcoats augmented our blankets to keep out the cold. It may have been the 'White Heat' of the Swingin' 60s, but the only source of heating was in the living room, and that was an open grate.

Payday was on Friday when I, then later with Shirley, was dispatched to the co-op with the boy's pram to do the weekly shop. It was a hard push back up to the Farm Gardens. Some Saturdays, I would have to go to the Grassmarket to purchase lentils, barley mix, porridge and broken biscuits all loose, and then bagged. Even with this cost-saving measure, and seven mouths to feed, hunger usually set in about Wednesday! Mum negotiated tick with the travelling shop, but she still managed, due to her Naval training, to magically rustle up hearty meals.

A dog appeared in our flat one day having attached itself to Ian and Keith, and then showed no sign of wishing to leave. Like our prefab dog, it was a loveable mutt adored by all. Especially friendly with strangers and sociable with other dogs, it unfortunately had one failing its love of balls, any size, any colour. Not until Kerry was satisfied that there was no life left in a ball, would he let go. Once the jaws were fastened, there was no release! He was another drain on household expenses, as people got to know where to come for recompense.

Interestingly, because the scheme was so new, there was only a Catholic Primary school available at Colinton Mains. It was crammed with the influx of baby boomers, of any faith until the new Primary was built. I never attended the new school as I was by then in Secondary at Firhill. I enjoyed arithmetic but struggled with spelling (still do). Practical subjects I particularly enjoyed, included cooking, sewing and dressmaking. In fact, one teacher would let me use the sewing machines during lunch breaks. I made quite a few skirts and dresses for myself; it made a change from hand-me-downs from a cousin. Susan, daughter of Mum's twin Freda, was tall and a fast-growing teenager, two years my senior. She stayed in the janitor's house at Kirkcaldy High School. Her father Jock, a retired sergeant major, was head Jannie.

I really enjoyed visiting, as Freda and Susan would take me shopping down in the town. I would often be treated to new pyjamas, underwear etc. While there, a joy was to have a long soak in the school baths hot and steamy. Such bliss compared to being fifth-in-line at the weekly kid's scrub, in the quickly cooling shared soap suds of Oxgangs.

An abiding memory of my high school years was the constant ribbing from my peers regarding my dress and shoes. Dad insisted on us all wearing boy's shoes (which he repaired), maintaining that they were more hard-wearing than girl's shoes. My hemlines were dropped several times and quite obvious. With two years left to attend school, Mum took up employment at the Dreghorn Barrack's kitchens. So, every school day I was dispatched, early mornings, with both brothers in tow to a creche in Polwarth. I then made for school, and depending on the regularity of Edinburgh Corporation Transport, was never sure of being on time for class.

A must, for all of us children, was the mandatory, regular Sunday visits to Granny Farquhar, Dad's mum. She would hold court with all the grandchildren she could cram into her Sighthill flat. This was after, should it be dry, walking through Colinton village, crossing the fields of Hailes farm, over the canal, on to Murrayburn and to Sighthill. Quite a trek for wee legs! If we were lucky, we might have the use of buses to get home. On rainy days, it was buses both ways, thank goodness. I was often allocated to her kitchen, involved in the sandwich making. In later years, Dad might take Kerry, on an evening, for an extended walk all the way to his mother's for a cuppa and a chat. Forever carried away with his blather, he would forget time. Granny would beg him to leave so as to catch his bus connections.

Even the dog's whine had no effect. After one such round trip, on arrival back at Oxgangs, Kerry lay down at the hearth, gave a huge sigh, and never woke up. Along with Kerry, and despite monetary privations, other animals began to appear mostly due to Shirley. To this day, she still harbours any ailing or needy pet. Her hamster was most obvious in its presence, shooting out from under the sofa giving Mum a start, interrupting her appreciation of something on TV. For a time, it set up home behind the gas cooker. With everyone fed up extricating it from whatever refuge it made after the escape, the combined belief was that hunger would drive it out. Not so, Mum's measurement of ingredients consisted of handfuls, from container to pot, with the resultant littering to await the next floor sweep. So, no food shortage for Hammy.

Later on, guinea pigs arrived but were banished to the back garden; Mum had put her foot down! Amazingly, Dad set about the construction of a hutch and run, soon necessary as it transpired that Shirley had no clue of the rodent's sexes with the resultant multiplication!

An aunt, Charlotte, the widow of Dad's brother Alex, was often thankful for my assistance around her house. Alex had been killed down the Pit. Her three children were still small, and having suffered a badly broken ankle, she struggled somewhat. She and her children stayed in a prefab, of which I was familiar, but at the Calders, close by the canal. I really enjoyed my stayovers there, for I was allowed to watch TV late. At home, at any sign of a close embrace or worse still, kissing, we were all sent to bed! Outer Limits, Twilight Zone and One Step Beyond were forbidden fruits. It was so easy since my bed was the living room sofa.

One night, I, half-sleeping, heard a light knocking on the front door. I inquired, "Who's there?" But to no response. I arose, made my way to the kitchen, only to be met with an unkempt, bearded face pressed to the window. Luckily, he made off into the night. Just as well, as a deeply snoring Charlotte could not be roused!

As her offspring advanced in years, my help was required less. Charlotte was yet another aunt who contributed to my wardrobe. The aforementioned (dropped hems) school skirt was purchased by her.

The only real spoiling I can recall was on holiday trips to the aforementioned Kirkaldy, but more especially to my would-be adoptive parents, the Bowers, firstly in Perth, then later their home territory of Inverness. On the outskirts of the (now) City of Inverness stood Drummond Towers, from where they ran a bed-and-breakfast establishment.

Mum would put me on the train at the Waverley with my little suitcase, and no doubt, juice and a snack for the long journey. Upon arrival, it was a car trip to the 'Towers' in Uncle Noel's car. Justine had knitted various garments for me, including a cardigan which I adored. She also made me dresses, and a nightgown which was pressed into service that very night. What with all that and the subsequent shopping expeditions, the homeward journey of my suitcase would contain little of what I'd departed with from Edinburgh!

Uncle Noel presented me with a rocking cradle he'd made, for the china doll I took a shine to from Cousin Joan's toy store under the stairs she was now a working adult in England. The beautiful doll, by the way, didn't last long. Within two weeks of return, I came home one day to find it in smithereens. The culprit, to this day, has never owned up. I would have lovely long lie-ins of a morning, as Auntie Justine had to see to the breakfasts of her paying guests. One day out shopping, a gent's voice rang out across the busy street. "Justine!" was the call, at which point I was hustled away. "It's your granddad," Auntie said. "Come away, he'll be looking for beer money." That was my one and only glimpse of Fred, my maternal grandfather. Luckily, a photograph remains to jog my memory.

Amongst all my granny trips to Sighthill, an abiding memory is one I'd rather not have at all. Somehow I got news of a youth club nearby. It was situated to the west of Calder Road, on what was mainly green space. These gatherings took place in a building that I assumed had some real use during WW2. Soft drinks, sweets and crisps were on sale. Pop music was played on a Dansette-type record player. Card games, table tennis, table football and the like were enjoyed.

It was, of course, a place to meet and socialise with others, and others I did meet. One handsome young fellow took a shine to me, asking for a date. Up to this time, I would quickly lose interest in chaps who all wanted to take me home to meet their mums!

Anyway, the next evening, I trotted back to meet up at the club, where he suggested a walk on the lovely warm summer evening. There were many paths on the Parkland where later the High Flats and Telford College (Sighthill) campus would be. At some point, we sat together on a grassy mound, and the usual teenage physicalities ensued.

I began to be aware that his snogging was becoming quite forceful, accompanied by heavy breathing. Now on top of me, it became obvious that no entrees or starters were on his menu; it was straight to the main course! I was shocked, but it didn't hinder me from trying to fight him off. Well! Thank goodness for dog walkers. Our struggling attracted a dog that rushed up, obviously thinking something exciting was afoot. Its owner, not wishing to upset our lover's tryst, called for its return. It, however, was not about to leave this 'game' and excitedly barked. That triggered a response in my attacker. He rolled off, and I legged it back to the main road.

Once aboard a corporation bus, I sat on the long bench side seat at the back of the lower saloon, near the conductor stationed on the back platform just as I had always been advised by Mum. Only when I perceived searching looks from him, did I realise the state I was in. Totally dishevelled with scratched knees and ripped nylons. I was more embarrassed at my appearance than at what had happened to me so recently. Sighthill Youth Club would no longer feature in my social calendar!

Chapter 5

School leaving was fast approaching and I was instructed to attend an interview in George Street, at the premises of Aitken and Niven, school outfitters. I then received a date to commence employment upon leaving school. I found it a pleasant place to work, with a good atmosphere amongst the staff. Looking forward to receiving my first pay packet, I was non-plussed to find my mum waiting at the shop door on my lunch break. I had to hand it over, was given back enough to cover bus fares and lunch monies. I could understand how difficult it was to feed a family of seven, but I'll admit to being rather miffed. The left-over cash seldom lasted long, and come the next week, it was a matter of begging for bus fares!

I was with Aitken and Niven for approximately six months, but, nice as they were, I found it all rather boring. Looking through the Situations Vacant columns of the *Edinburgh Evening News*, I espied an advertisement seeking apprentice juniors in hairdressing. This was to be at Jenners, the city's most prestigious department store. To be indentured required the guarantee of either parents or guardians. Since any such employment would mean a huge drop in earnings, there was no point in approaching Dad. Having convinced Mum of my earnestness, and with her enthusiastic encouragement, it was an immediate neighbour who came to the rescue. Mrs Mac asked to be provided with a sample of Jimmie's signature, and indeed it was she who signed on the dotted line!

So, with parental consent and having had a successful interview, I was now to work in Jenners. It was quite a revelation just how old-fashioned it still was. Modern salons, as we still know them today, were in full swing it was, after all the 'Swingin' 60s.' However, Jenner's Hair Salon was more like the 1860s! Not even cubicles, but individual exclusive rooms, each with their own door for privacy. Thankfully, plans were in place to modernise at the time I started.

Within six months, the beautifully panelled old rooms were swept away, and the now open-plan floor was leased out to Jacque Dessange of Paris, a London-based company. The wrinkly, grey-haired old lady, who I passed up pins and rollers to—she was no more. Big changes now with many nationalities, all male, and seemingly all with French names!

Monsieur Georges (Greek!) left hand was missing half of two fingers. These he utilised to form pin curls! He was though, an excellent stylist and appreciated by his many clients. He blotted his copybook, however, by developing a fixation on one particular client. One day, he just wasn't there, and the whispered tale was that he'd been recalled back to London Headquarters. Msr. Georges was forever wanting me to cut my shoulder-length auburn hair, but the visiting Manageress from London said she was quite happy with it, as it was always tidy and well groomed. I did eventually cut it shorter, but only to achieve the 'in' hairdo of the day; the Beehive! Surely the highest maintenance style, ever. What with the early morning repairs after a deep sleep? Plus the crushing effect of a crash helmet if on a motorcycle ride.

Monsieur Pierre (German!) was the replacement for the errant Georges, a likeable chap equally popular with staff and client alike, and again, an excellent stylist. His departure was due to a junior member of staff becoming pregnant. Popular with her too, it would seem! Yet another replacement arrived. Monsieur Michel (Tunisian!) was always of good humour, very expressive and flamboyant and always immaculate in suit and tie.

Equally flamboyant, but in a more masculine manner, were two actual French guys. They remained throughout most of my training. They had a habit of always being late, and then proceeding to have breakfast on the premises, usually sharing a French stick with smelly cheese. Not being employees of Jenners, they to our chagrin got away with it. The techniques they used were new to us in that they would set the hair in rollers, dry it under a hood drier. We would then remove the rollers. A hand drier and a brush were utilised, brushing out the roller marks. This created body and lift for the styling.

The average number of stylists was five, aided and abetted by one receptionist, four juniors and one improver (soon to be qualified). Plus an elderly lady whose duties were many and various towel washing, drying, stacking, general cleaning of the salon and staffroom. When not on the salon floor, she could always be observed with a cigarette hanging, dead centre, between her lips. Mary was a real character, and of an evening, would hold court while serving in the Grand Circle Bar of the King's Theatre. Work-shy, she was not!

Despite all the modernisation and new designer fittings and decor, a goodly percentage of our clientele were still loyal ladies of advancing years. The shampoo and set, blue rinse brigade. An amusement for the French duo, always inducing giggles, was the ladies forgetting they were no longer in private cubicles. Slumber might overtake them while under the bank of driers, with a resultant relaxing. It was easy then to check out the colour and texture of the voluminous bloomers, which were still being worn by part of Edinburgh's elite.

My work at Jenners was quite varied; in fact, I think the training covered just about every aspect of hair care. It was such that in future employment I never had to do a trial hairdo, which was the norm. One stylist thought I should specialise in colouring, but I vetoed that idea. I loved every minute of my job despite the rather rigid rules. Distraction was not tolerated, and I recall the old school knuckle-rapping admonition should I become inattentive with a comb, not a ruler I might add!

One part of the salon was still partitioned off for clients shy of others knowing the secrets of their treatments. It was also used for wig fittings, with the styling of the same on wig blocks. One process I thought that came out of the Ark was the treatment of clients with hair loss. The person would have to hold, in each hand, an electrified glass rod. The current was switched on, and I would have to be quick applying my fingers to her scalp, as I might receive more than a tingle! Whether it made a bit of difference I know not. *The client knows best* was the adage, but to this day, I still cannot quite figure out why a time-ravaged countenance would wish to be framed with the locks of a young gypsy girl!

My Auntie Justine, when she heard of my Jenner's job, came to the rescue yet again. She ensured I was clad in the staff overalls, mandatory in their employ. They, of course, were required to be top quality and were not cheap. Just as well at apprentice rates starting at £1-10/-, rising to £5 after three years. As previously mentioned, the drop in earnings was not appreciated by my dad. He maintained that I should contribute more to the home finances, and having taken this course, was no longer welcome under his roof. Funnily enough, it was his mother who offered a solution—accommodation with her.

Knowing her house intimately, I looked forward to a bed of my own, a room on my own. No such luck, it would seem I was required to share her double bed, me nearest the wall! It transpired that she had the measure of her youngest son, a Merchant Seaman, and this arrangement ensured propriety. She did appreciate my assistance sometimes, helping undo the laces of her stays! Latterly, she was the head dinner lady at Tynecastle School, but retired by this time.

I became aware at some point that there were always part-time evening jobs coming up, in theatres and cinemas. So in an attempt to bolster my meagre finances, I was on the lookout. I soon found an opening at the Caley Picture House in Lothian Road. This was a really enjoyable period in my life, showing people to their seats, 'shushing' the noise with a flash of my torch and selling ice cream from the shoulder-hung tray down by the big silver screen. Later, a sweetie shop opened in the foyer, also a hot dog stand. More significantly, however, it was where I met my future husband. He was employed as a projectionist, up beneath the roof, showing the films. While we were both 'attached' at our first encounter, we clicked immediately and were soon an 'item.'

Besides the regular film shows, there were sometimes special events. One I'll never forget was a Sunday afternoon showing of a London boxing match of the previous evening, filmed, immediately processed and dispatched through the night to certain cinemas nationwide, one of which was the Caley. The cinema was packed out and the other girls had not turned out. I never made as much money selling ice cream ever again! With the match over and the cinema emptied, I was still trying to square the takings against sales. John McGloughlin, the owner was by now wishing to close the doors and enquired after my tribulations. He said, "Never mind, Carol, the girls will sort it tomorrow." Sort it they did, as it became obvious that they were all on the take, and they hadn't yet thought to include me!

The construction of a narrow stage in front of the curtained proscenium was the harbinger of a new Festival Caley event. Late-night concerts. The folk group the CORRIES hired the cinema for the duration of the festival. After the film show, a quick litter-clearing was carried out, before re-opening the doors to folk fans. Eleven o'clock saw the duo bound up the steps and onto the stage to rapturous applause.

A crowd-pleasing sing-along kicked off the show. The lads then introduced the guest band/entertainer, leaving when the act joined them on stage. There was much contrast in the entertainment, what with such diverse talents as the McAlmans (excellent), and Ravi Shankar (sleep-inducing). During the intermission, ice creams etc. were on sale. Then down went the lights once more, for Roy and Ronnie who provided a good 45 minutes plus of their distinctive style of folk music. At the concert end, the boss had corporation buses, hired and waiting, early hours, to convey all the staff home.

Courting proved somewhat difficult, what with the last buses departing the city centre prior to eleven o'clock. Having been seen 'home' to Grannie's at Sighthill, the buses all went, part route to Longstone depot, three or four stops along Calder Road.

With no dosh for taxis and a night bus not due till nearer one am, it was Shank's pony for Erik. He was, at that time, lodging at Union Place. Later, he got a bedsit in Newington even further to walk. He always said he didn't mind but was a bit miffed as he seldom got 'a good snog,' (his words!). This was because Grannie's radar was so good, we were no sooner in the stairwell than came the call, "Is that you, Carol? Get up this stair now." Well! and me a seventeen-year-old.

On my suggestion, he asked his landlord about bedsit availability, as he in fact had three properties on the south side. So, I was really pleased when I took up residence in a room in Newington quite close to my boyfriend. Life was much easier from then on. My own place!

The Beehive (Photo: Erik Young, Projectionist)

Erik Young (Photo: Tam Kerr)

Chapter 6

St. Johns Vestry (Photo: Author's collection)

My apprenticeship contract as a junior was fast approaching completion, after the statutory three years. I was then offered the chance to specialise as a colourist for the next two years of improving. A pay rise of fl-10/- was offered! I handed in my notice immediately. An opening in Leith presented itself at Coiffure la Fayre, in Great Junction Street. With no mention of improving, I was, through my Jenner's training, straight to work as a stylist! My £6-10/- offered in Princes Street shot up to £12!

The salon belonged to a butcher who had a business nearby, but he employed a stylist of experience to manage the shop. An experience I had not come across came my way one day when a mother asked me to cut off most of her daughter's lovely long hair. I was really quite sorry for the girl as I thought her hair just needed a trim, and to be shorn seemed a bit harsh. On their departure, I swept up the cuttings, and as I transferred them to the bin I realised that her dandruff was in fact nits! The girl's mum had not indicated this to me. I was mortified and the boss was livid as all equipment had to be deep-cleaned and sterilised, the last thing you need in a busy salon. Not in my lifetime had I any experience of such a thing.

I was soon keen to move on as the promised commission never materialised, even though I was happy enough there. So, job seeking was once more on my agenda after a period of approximately six months.

Salon Henry were looking for stylists about this time, and an appointment was made for a trial. I arrived at their Tollcross salon and was about to start when Mrs Hen(d)ry arrived and chatted with me. Upon hearing of my training, she told her stylist, "That won't be necessary. When can you start?"

I was eighteen years old when Erik and I decided to get engaged, one year into our courtship. We planned to marry the following year. Sometime after our first meeting, he realised the extent of my wardrobe asking, "Is that your only coat?" Well, it was, so he took me to Paige on Princes Street, and bought me a lovely camelhair coat. He was in a better-paying job by this time with NCR, involving the maintenance and repair of cash registers and accounting machines.

When it came to putting up the Banns in the church, birth certificates were required and I got a copy from Mum. To my absolute surprise, it stated that my surname was Mackenzie, Mum's maiden name, and not in fact Farquhar. It was obvious that I was never officially adopted. To think I had to suffer as a child, all the 'F' names you might think of relating to my given name.

In late January 1969, we were married at the Church of Saint Johns in Oxgangs. Nowadays, you can worship at the altar of consumerism in Aldi's, as the Kirk is no more! The Rev Orr took the service, and after this, we repaired to the Cairn Hotel in Windsor Street for the reception, to be joined by more work colleagues adding to all the relatives who attended. Sadly, my mum couldn't witness the event as she was very unwell at this time. None of Erik's family attended as, before oil, wages in the Isles were poor and they couldn't afford the travel and accommodation.

The 'going away' was a taxi to the Caledonian Hotel, with a planned next-day BEA flight to Shetland. A plan B was required as no planes were flying due to a baggage handler's strike. So, after our honeymoon night, it was back to Erik's bedsit. Come the Monday, it was the train to Aberdeen, followed by the steamer voyage overnight, crossing some of Britain's roughest waters. As we sailed out of the basin that evening, we sat at the captain's table in first class. Over the harbour bar, the St Clair rose then fell.

I looked apprehensively at my new husband. I needn't have worried, for it was mirror calm for the 180-mile trip. Our honeymoon coincided with the Up-Helly Aa Fire Festival. I truly had never seen the like. The burning was followed by a whole night of dancing and revelry. I began to wilt about 3 am and we returned to my in-laws flat in the historic south end of Lerwick. The following Friday, my husband's parents laid on a Hamefaerin (welcome home) as a second reception complete with another cake. Again lots of dancing and meeting up with Erik's friends and relations.

All too soon, it was back to Edinburgh and work. Rather than pay rent, we went looking for a flat to buy. We settled on a Leith tenement, second-floor room, toilet and kitchen. No mortgage was required as easy instalments were offered. Erik was always busy improving the place.

After having a stove fitted, he surrounded it with a long mantel, plus shelving complete with a drop-down record player. A room divider followed sectioning off the tiny sink/cooker area. In the bedroom, he constructed a shower, disguised as a wardrobe. For the first year, we slept on a collapsible settee!

Hearing of my move, Mrs Hendry suggested I transfer to Davidson's Mains salon, as it was a direct connection by bus. The atmosphere there was much more relaxed, with Mr Jack as head stylist/manager. I was one of four stylists who appreciated the assistance of a local old lady, Effie, with the cleaning, floor-sweeping, towels etc., and the endless cups of tea or coffee. The appointments were kept quite tight and if anybody fell behind, assistance was quickly offered. Some money went through that till, and Mrs Hendry's daughter called along shortly before closing to empty it.

Mr Jack's clients used to spoil him with gifts, and as his holidays approached, his tips were huge. We girls never got big tips, always the guys just as it was in Jenners, irrespective of being quite often better than them. We girls used to perm Mr Jack's hair, long before it became a footballer's must-have style the Kevin Keegan look.

I remained working at 'D' Mains till I was well through a pregnancy with my first child. Once word was out some of the girls got their mums to knit for a baby. I got two lovely suits, jackets and leggings, with hats and mittens to match.

While always delighted to welcome visitors to our home, there were those we weren't so keen on. After Hubby formed a window shelf in the living room with sliding doors below, food storage problems were alleviated. Turned out, it was a magnet for mice that, up till then, had been quite happy residing in the flat below. Sitting watching TVe one evening, Mummy and Daddy Mouse decided to introduce their brood of three to us marching in line along the long hearth slabs! War was immediately declared, Erik reducing their number over successive evenings with a trap in the window cupboard; cornflakes the lure. All, bar Daddy Mouse, were caught and dispatched. He, however, proved wily hoovering up the cereal, but ignoring the trap.

One evening, Hubby was tapping away on an ancient typewriter placed on the couch; him sitting on the pouffe. I was at the cooker, both of us oblivious to any presence. Out of the corner of his eye, Erik observed Daddy Mouse watching intently. He chased Daddy Mouse all around the room until he shot inside Hubby's Cuban-heeled zip boot under the couch. Quick as a flash, he grabbed the boot tight and shot out of the room. Upon his return, and hearing the loo flush, I enquired after the mouse, to be told, "He's on a long swim, all the way to Seafield!" (Edinburgh city's sewage farm).

Chapter 7

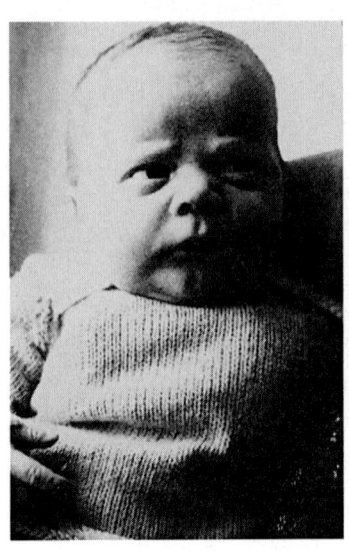 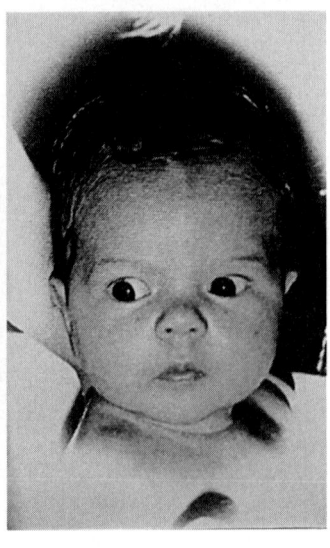

Darren   *Erika Young*

(Photos: Doughlas Bentlay)

(Photos: Doughlas Bentlay)

Two weeks overdue, I was painting a chest of drawers for the baby, when I was ordered into the Eastern General for inducing. Well! What a marathon; this baby was content to stay where it was. My labour lasted 24 hrs, and poor Hubby was drained with lack of sleep and anxiety. No birth would he witness, as he was ushered out by a surgeon clad in a floor-length rubber apron and wellie boots! When Erika was born, she was jaundiced and required special attention and monitoring in a controlled environment. Erik's first glimpse of his new daughter was through the glass partition of the unit. With her yellow complexion and jet-black hair, he made a comment of a possible liaison with an Oriental gentleman! Always quick with the quips—that I had to get used to. The black hair disappeared, to be replaced with colouring more a match of her dad's. I could see that she was, in fact, like her Auntie Peggy, Erik's big sister. With the new baby being kept under observation, the length of separation was considerable. By the time we were reunited, any chance of breast feeding was gone. I was really disappointed missing out on the initial bonding.

Soon we were all together in our cosy Graham Street flat. About six months later, a woman came knocking at the door, she had heard on the grapevine of my being a hairdresser. Her husband, who had the Chipshop just up from the Bonnington Bridge, had set her up in hairdressing just next to Sandy, the newsagent. Until she built up staff and trade, she asked if I might help out on Fridays and Saturdays. She would watch Erika on a Friday, and on a Saturday, Erik took on that job. On the odd occasion, my mum would come across town from Oxgangs, and take her granddaughter out in the pram, and spoil her. The Viccy Park was a favourite with her.

The salon owner had a huge St Bernard dog, such a peaceable animal. It loped over to Erika, sitting in her

McLaren buggy by the door. She extended her little arm to greet the dog, only to see it disappear into its cavernous jaws! A facelicking would follow, leaving Erika spluttering. It felt good, though, keeping my hand in, and with a few quid in that hand.

During this time Erik left NCR, as the future was electronic—he was more mechanical-minded. He started, as a temporary measure, conducting, and then driving buses with Edinburgh Corporation Transport. As these involved shifts, I could no longer help out at the Street-end salon, but it was enjoyable while it lasted. It also helped me get to know some of the locals. I was, by this time, already pregnant again. When baby number two was born, just over 19 months after the first, it was thankfully without drama. He, Darren, just popped out! An Elsie's baby, he was as peaceable as the aforementioned St Bernard.

Post-natal, we were grouped; six beds, with breastfeeding, we were expected to write up our charts, with quantity and frequency. This proved problematic as Darren, after latching on and two sucks, would promptly go back to sleep. On one occasion, I too fell asleep, and waking had no clue what progress had been made, as yet again he was in slumberland. I had to tickle his feet to wake him. He would open his eyes, smile, and have his two sucks and then back to sleep yet again! My only recourse was to 'cook the books' with my bed-end chart.

Things were now getting a bit crowded in our little flat, so it was put on the market. A deal was done, for double what we'd paid, and we started looking for property. When Darren was about four months a solicitor's letter popped through our door. Bad news! The buyers, who were delighted with our improved premises, were in no hurry to conclude the missives they had pulled out. Erik phoned the agents to be told, 'Read your Evening News.' The front page news was that the new labour administration, with its leader Jack (citizen) Kane, had announced a major clearance of what they deemed substandard housing in the city. Included in the list was Graham Street! Apparently, a new Jerusalem in social housing was to be built on the very same farmland my family used to traverse on Granny Sundays – Haile's farm. This would carry the name Wester Hailes.

Erik saw this as a body-blow, as our flat overnight was worthless. He found out that, back home, drivers were required, and having his PSV a job was guaranteed. He decided, and as a dutiful wife (!), I concurred that we might have a stab at island living. Erik set about advertising every stick of furniture, people viewed; he then hired a van to deliver these items to the addresses provided and cash on delivery. Having posted spare keys through the letter box, we overnighted with various relatives, and the next day were at Turnhouse expecting to fly to Shetland.

With just our clothing in suitcases, plus a baby buggy, we were given the news at check-in that Sumburgh was Fogbound, and they had no wish to accept our flight tickets. Erik said that as a Sheltie he knew that sea fog could disappear in minutes, and anyway we were effectively homeless! With reluctance, the BEA staff issued us with our boarding passes, and soon we were airborne heading north via Aberdeen. We had no wailing baby on board to upset other passengers, for wee Darren, as was his wont, was interested in all around. After a session at the breast, it was peaceful sleep thereafter. As we taxied to a halt on the apron at Dyce, an announcement addressing Shetland passengers, requested that they identify their luggage on the trucks so it could be reloaded once more it seemed that Sumburgh was now fog-free! In fact, we arrived in the most beautiful sunshine.

We were met off the Airways bus by Erik's dad, and together, we all walked the relatively short distance to the flat at Stout's Court. Darren had to be carried as Erik omitted the buggy retrieval in the stramash air-side at ABZ. In some ways, we felt like refugees as we trudged along Lerwick's flagstone streets. Helpfully, my in-laws took us in till we found a home for our family. Hopefully, we wouldn't have to over-stay our welcome. The very next day, Erik was at the wheel with Leasks of Lerwick coaches.

In less than two months, a local hairdresser came knocking, asking if I might help out in his salon as there was a dearth of stylists. All trainee hairdressers now had to attend colleges (polytechnics) on the mainland. I placed Erika in a playgroup in the mornings but of course, Darren was too wee. "No problem," said Peter Black. The wife could look after Darren for the few hours that I'd work. I was quite taken aback by some really old-fashioned practices there, but everyone was very friendly. Just as well, as being up-rooted from a city environment I did feel a bit like a duck out of water.

Oil had been discovered in the seas around Shetland, and there was talk of a klondyke. Every now and then a stranger would walk down the gangplank off the Aberdeen ferry, looking for who knows what? One such came my way at Peter's salon for a shampoo and set. She might best be described as possibly a 'Lady of the night.' She got my best attention, then asked for the toilet. She then emerged from the loo with an obvious wig pulled on over my work! I mentioned this to Peter whose response was perhaps it was a disguise and anyway she'd paid.

A week or so later, she sailed away, the Constabulary ensuring her departure at the quayside. Not without her shouting her feelings to the assembled pier-head crowd, to the effect that the local women were all of her calling, but gave it for free!

Erik was soon poached from Leasks by his two cousins who operated the transport fleet in the village of Scalloway, seven miles west of Lerwick. A higher wage was offered, plus the promise of a working partnership. A car was provided for the to and fro. This was to be our norm for some considerable time. Also the norm, unfortunately, was our living environment, since all four of us were squeezed into one room—bunk beds and a double bed. Every Monday morning after ferrying Scalloway workers to town, and with a one-and-a-half-hour lie-over, Erik would visit the council housing officer. He informed me their chats went well, but it would be sixteen months before we, at last, were granted let of 6, Blydoit, Scalloway walking distance from the bus depot.

The wooden-clad house was of kit form imported from Norway and, as one would expect, was top quality. I loved the house and its location, with a lovely view across the East Voe to Scalloway's ancient castle. The timing of our rental was almost karma, as we had only just received a settlement from Edinburgh Corporation in lieu of compulsory purchase regarding 13, Graham Street. It wasn't a huge figure, being midway between the purchase cost and our, hoped-for, sale price. Still, it carpeted the whole house, with some, in vogue, furniture from Habitat.

With no transport of my own, I was now a stay-at-home mum. I didn't mind in the least, but it didn't take long for the phone to ring with potential clients. So as not to cause worries regarding the conditions of let, I was quick to suggest that if one could provide their home and round up a few friends also, a discount for their hairdo would be a consideration. I was picked up with Darren and my gear, and would often spend a busy but enjoyable 1/2 day—with a few quid at the end of it.

One day in the bathroom, I think I fainted. Erik came rushing to find me on the floor. He sat me up, apparently, and then just at my eyebrow a cut started pouring blood. It seems I had given the bath a head-butt. The doctor in Scalloway at that time was a brusque, ex-services medic. He breezed in that Sunday, to enquire of my husband, "Bit of a domestic, Erik?" Talk about mortified—poor Erik! Birth control was yet another story. Later on, another doctor, a tall lugubrious chap who looked well past retiral, was not forthcoming with any expected recommendation. Living the (Ahem!) life of any young couple, we were finding it expensive with Erik's regular visits to the Pharmacy. Across the surgery desk, he suggested to me that we should employ the method he and his good lady had used for many years... Prayer!

I was soon popular with the Shetland ladies and began to think I should set up in business. The search for premises to rent in Lerwick was without success. It was a case of whatever we saw, an enquiry always got the response; not hairdressing as they would not like to rock-the-boat, and upset existing businesses! I was even more determined as a result. We found and purchased derelict premises just off the main street, up a lane, and applied for planning permission. No help was forthcoming from the Highland and Islands Development

Board (HIDB). They stated that there was a sufficiency in island haircare, with three ladies' salons and two barbers in town—for an Isles population of around 21,000!

Other than an abortive foray into the then-unlicensed taxi hire business after the promised partnership never materialised, Erik returned to the bus work. Back with Leasks, he then got word of a driving job with the pioneers at Sullom Voe. He'd pick up staff in Lerwick and Scalloway, and transport them to Calback Ness. The rest of the day, he was back in Lerwick, sourcing items for the various firms involved working the site of what would become Europe's largest oil terminal. Life at home carried on as before, except that the kids only saw their dad at the go-to-bed time. He started at 0530 and got home at 1930—seven days a week! The money was good though and we were able to build up a fund for the hoped-for salon. After ten months, he'd had it, which was just as well as it was time to redevelop our lane property.

Forever surrounded by a wild variety of colourful Fair Isle jumpers, I felt inspired to take up knitting again. My school years gave me the basics in this skill, and I was soon back in the groove of 'Maakin'—a Shetlandic term. Erik's mum was a most excellent knitter and passed on quite a few tips, especially when I first attempted Fair Isle garments.

Erik had previously warned me that the Isles were 'Gansey territory!' (Guernsey). Yet another word I had to get used to. I also learned that a jumper was sometimes called a 'Joopie'.

Cold winter blasts were experienced by the young Blydoit kids marching to school, so I was soon knitting a balaclava for Darren. Boy! Did he love that particular item of clothing?

One night before retiring, looking in on our sleeping brood, I was amazed to find him sound asleep in his pyjama ensemble having the addition of his balaclava! I had to wake him up to peel it off, then towel his soaking curls.

City girl in Lerwick, Shetland (Photo: Erik Young)

Chapter 8

A relative back in Edinburgh was just completing his joiner apprenticeship, but not particularly looking forward to a lifetime of screwing school desks together, or the constant tarting up of the city's bars. The prospect of being involved in the complete strip out and rebuild of 5/7 Reform Lane appealed since it would cover almost every aspect of the building. Soon he would join us in the venture. With Erik now no longer on the buses, and having purchased a small truck, they both got stuck in with gutting the premises.

I meantime headed up to the worker's camp of Firth, near Sullom Voe. Chambermaid duties cleaning the terminal builders' accommodations would add to our building funds and home expenses.

There were quite a few rooms requiring cleaning every day, with weekly bed changing. It was satisfying work but with no slacking. I recall one slacker though, a local, she was quite the party girl, out till early hours. The resultant room care was decidedly below par on her block. One chap was sure that she was sleeping on the job. He checked a mate's room in the adjoining block and realised how spotless and clean it was. He remedied the situation, leaving an obvious message to her, by shaking Talcum powder all over his room! From then on, she spent a lot less time kipping on his bed.

The lads were not long into the project when a chance for temporary premises came my way. It was at the now-empty, infant school on King Harald Street. So building work moved to the playground huts, with partitioning, wiring, plumbing etc. The idea of the Council Development Department was as a start-up stepping stones for small businesses. This meant I could set up in self-employed hairdressing much sooner since wee Darren would be but two minutes away at the nursery in the main school building. Across the hall from me was an electrical wizard, Mr Henderson. It seemed that there was nothing he couldn't fix. He had a full-size classroom to himself, but it didn't take long for it to fill up with repaired items that were never collected!

Progress on the salon in the lane was steady, and come August 1978, I moved from the school huts. Not, though, before giving a party on the new premises, with family, friends and near neighbours. Canapes, Fizz, and other delights were on offer, and Mr Irvine the Horologist opposite presented me with a wall clock for the salon. Having had the use of the classroom I was able to transfer to Reform Lane with a full appointment book!

Changes now for my builders. Erik was back up at Sullom Voe, big buses this time, for another eight-month stint. Our joiner returned to Edinburgh with a cash bonus, on top of his duration expenses—also with a driving licence. His test on roads having only one set of traffic lights and instruction from a certain Mr Gifford!

I loved my new salon and the realisation finally overtook me, I had my own business at last I was my own boss! I had advertised for a shampooist/assistant prior to the move and was joined by Winnie who proved to be a great help. Darren was now of school age so I had no worries on the childcare front. He trooped off up the Mill Brae in the care of his big sister, joining the little band of Blydoit children. When Erik had enough of Sullom Voe, he was back with Georgeson and Moore in Scalloway. His oil money soon paid off the building expenses owing to Hay and Co.

Term breaks from the technical colleges meant phone calls from trainees looking for work experience. I had several along the way. While they were expected to be unpaid, per instructions from the college, I couldn't not pay for work done. Especially as it meant my right hand (Winnie) could get her holidays. Later on, Maureen came next as my assistant and was an equally great help. Two trainees who were exceptional were coincidentally from the Island of Whalsay—but at different times of course. Jo was a very good artist who painted pictures of fishing boats, for their owners from that fishing community. Odette, a very good hairdresser, was incidentally the granddaughter of Nancy, my very first home-hairdressing client. Odette's mum and Auntie Helene used to bring her, as a child, for her haircuts. Perhaps she enjoyed my attention, and that gave her the notion for a hairdressing career.

One regular client, Margaret the Fishmonger, asked if I might consider employing another stylist. She knew of a family moving to the Isles, the young man of whom was indeed a hairdresser from an English city. Erik altered the Mezzanine waiting area with a two-station section. Clifford was certainly good at what he did; it was just the time he took to do it. He was as laid-back as his Jamaican ancestry might dictate!

Hours overtook earnings, and I was forced to phone clients' employers to indicate that their lateness was due to their hair attention detention! Mercifully, it transpired that island living was not for the family, and they soon departed. That saved me from delivering the no-longer-required sermon.

During the conversion of 5/7, the construction of the staircase by our joiner coincided with the school holidays. The kids now were to miss out on our usual go-away trips, but Erik was undeterred and planned a getaway locally. Off to Islesburgh, he went, hiring tents, sleeping bags, etc. from Harold Leask. After checking on any building requirements, we left our craftsman to his task.

We loaded up the pickup truck with all the camping gear and set off through Nesting, and just past Newing, we set up camp down by the shore. Erik and the kids were in their element, but it's really something I can do without. Previous family holidays had expanded our horizons to the South of England, and beyond—the Isle of Wight. Static caravans were the reasonably priced options. This holiday certainly was not up to those standards. Continental holidays were becoming even more likely, with being in charge of our own finances. Still, when those did come along we were usually still paying back the bank come Christmas! Dumping children on grandparents at holiday time, then swanning off to do your own thing was never in our minds. In any case, Erik's folks had more than been of help when we arrived on Shetland's shores.

Our little camping expedition didn't provide us with any measure of solitude. First along were, quite rightly, the tenant crofters checking us out. They gave us their blessing stating, "Better you than us!" Cars passing along the quiet highway would often sound their horns, requiring us to wave. One night while abed, we heard a car slow and then stop. Only two reasons were appropriate in the circumstance; one, the call of nature; two, a visitation. Whispered voices drew close and their intention was clear – unclipping the guy ropes. "Don't you dare!" Erik yelled. Young Mr Mouat, son of the local postman, his pal and two girlfriends introduced themselves.

Erik broke out the red wine box and got life back into the campfire embers. Red tins soon appeared; conversation and laughter then continued around the blazing driftwood till near three o'clock, as the Shetland dawn became obvious. Our only other regular visitor was a lonely seal, who seemed intrigued by our presence.

The business had settled into a rhythm if not quite a well-oiled machine. I would see the kids out the door to school, and then drive into Lerwick for a 0930 opening time. 'Drive' is certainly one way to put it, as my vehicles were never top dollar. My driving test I had passed two years previously while still a stay-at-home mum, after instruction from that certain Mr Gifford.

Erik got a cheap Fiat for my running about. Other than a badly slipping clutch, and whiskering plugs (which I learned to remove and clean!), it ran very well. I was assured by my Hubbie that the grinding of brakes was only to be expected given the car's vintage. Coming down Knab Road one day, I braked at the Annsbrae giveaway, only to hear a crunch, and then lost all braking ability! Church Road and the harbour beyond then beckoned. I sailed across the junction (no other traffic thankfully), mounted the kerb and utilised the low dyke at St Olaf's Hall as a…stop!

Swiftly replaced, the Fiat was sold into Unst, and a Hillman Avenger was now my transport. Erik quickly replaced a dropped valve spring, and then she indeed ran very well. She didn't take kindly, however, to the Isle's salty atmosphere as rust, and molecular deterioration overcame her. Later in my ownership, she was ahead of the game in any two-tone colour trend, ending up with her bright blue bodywork enhanced with two doors, boot lid and bonnet in deep maroon!

Reform Lane, Lerwik, Shetland (Photos: Erik Young)

Chapter 9

Part of Erik's duties at Georgeson and Moore was transporting the Nesting/Girlsta and Tingwall children to Scalloway Junior High. Erik always had a soft spot for Nesting, having enjoyed childhood summer holidays at Catfirth. A council house became available at Stendaal and we went for it. It also made sense in regard to the school run, as the bus could remain in Nesting overnight meaning only one round trip rather than two as previously. All our possessions were heaped on Johnson's flatbed lorry and off we went on our next adventure.

Number 18 was perhaps not as good a house as the Nordic, but it was pleasant enough, with lovely views across the Voe of Vassa. Erik moored his boat mid-voe. He would always be looking and checking on her. The kids settled in well, apart from (thankfully) only one bully at the little two-teacher school. The local kids all got on very well and would roam and explore to their heart's content. On their pushbikes, they would 'do the loop' Vassa, Skellister and Catfirth round. Sometimes down to the Quoys burn, a lovely spot to explore.

One day as I watched the children play from my kitchen window, I observed one young lass eating earth! Not only that, she would pop round stones into her mouth, sometimes licking them clean with her tongue! She grew up to be a very attractive young lady who is a whizz at landscape photography. Her grandmother was a school cook, and to this day, our kids aver that her meals were the best ever!

Not long after we took up residence, new tenants arrived immediately next door, the Frasers. Tea and biscuits we offered them, and they became very good neighbours indeed. Such that come Christmastime, their house became our Santa store. Their boys were now too big to believe. One time I sent Erik through to collect Santa pressies. He seemed to take forever so I went to investigate. A rather special Brandy was involved, and my hubby was almost legless. Bill apologised to me saying, "We're still waiting for that star in the East!"

The Frasers had a lovely, peaceable German Shepherd dog, much given to flatulence. This gave the family Cart Blanche to suffer no such discomfort, but immediately scold her with a 'Neula, really!' She would look up enquiringly as if to ask, "Was that really me?"

One evening sitting watching TV, me knitting, a loud knock at the door was immediately followed by the blue boilersuited image of Kenneth McKay in our living room. In my direction, he flung a furry ball, which on landing used every claw it had to attach itself to my bosom. "It's the last one," he said. "If you don't want her, she's in the Voe…damn house cat's kettled again!" With no other option, she stayed. The name Pussy-kins soon morphed into Pushkin, and so it remained. A most attractive Tabby it had, though, some unusual traits—let me out; no, let me in, with the accompanying meowing. At Stendaal, it wasn't a problem as we and Erika slept upstairs, Darren had a small bedroom on the ground floor. He usually drifted off to sleep listening to cassette tapes through large cushioned earphones, impervious to any caterwauling at his window.

One time as I drove to work, I developed an itching; only remembering that Pushkin had been out all night in the hill, not at the windows. I assumed an encounter with wildlife, most probably rabbits, was the cause of my discomfort. Luckily, soon after starting work, Erik popped in, I dropped the comb and scissors and propelled him to the WC by the main door. Quickly stripping to the waist, to his remark, "Could this not have been last night?" I begged him to assist in the removal of my unwanted guests. He picked and squashed, picked and squashed, while I went over my garments with eagle eyes. I prayed that none had jumped to any of my clients. Previously, Erika had developed a rash, so it was off to the doctor. "Any wildlife or pets?" He enquired. So, it was flea powder application, much to Pushkin's discomfiture.

More strange behaviour followed at a later date heralding Pushkin's own 'kettling'. Fussing about, wanting out, but not wanting out and quite unsettling, really. Finally, she disappeared for some time. A search was carried out only to find her in Erika's bedroom cupboard, in her doll's pram, with two little Tabbys (one with white socks), and another, black and white but sadly still. Erik quickly removed the stillborn, found a strong cardboard box, cut a deep 'V' for access plopped Pushkin's favourite old jumper in the box along with her little brood.

Motherhood came naturally to her but, yet again, another strange trait became apparent. Whenever she rounded up the kittens for the box and suckled, she just stood and meowed at them! We never once witnessed the natural pick-up-by-neck routine. We had to do it for her. Once the kittens got their legs and climbing ability it ceased to be a problem. When they were of an age to adopt we advertised on the teatime BBC Radio Shetland. Tabby No.1 (female) went off to the West Side. Tabby No.2 (male) white socks went to Hamnavoe to a client. He took to her husband and would drape himself around his neck while he watched TV. Sadly, he didn't survive an encounter with a fast car near the Public Hall.

I had by this time much better transport. The Council Social Services were dishing out mobility vehicles all over, I assume with oil money. The little orange Volvo 66 was to be seen all around the Isles. The three-year was up on one, and I got it at a good price. It was a dream on the snow and ice. Just as well as in those days, only quarry dust was used as road grit come winter time. Many a trip I made, to and from town in such circumstances, but I never had a bit of bother. Constantly variable gearing—I was reliably informed.

One such quick dash I had to make with the 66 was to and from the Brae Surgery. Erika had been complaining of stomach pain for several days, and no remedy seemed to alleviate her increasing agony. It had all the symptoms of being a stitch—but all the time? Upon examination, Dr Clubb diagnosed appendicitis and commanded she be taken immediately to the Gilbert Bain Hospital, his phone call preceding our arrival. What a day we chose, as the oil industry, healthcare and all emergency services were put on high alert. They didn't want to admit Erika, but we insisted on Dr Clubb's advice. Later on, hours later, she was finally taken to the theatre. The so-called emergency had been nought, but an exercise. Our agonised, bent double little girl was in a gangrenous state—high-risk Peritonitis. Apparently no one, other than those at the 'Top,' knew it was an exercise. A strong letter of complaint appeared in the *Shetland Times*, and probably in the Health Board's In Tray, penned by the GB's own head anaesthetist.

Poor Erika was abed at the hospital for a week, then confined to the house for another. But, bless her, she made a full if slow recovery. Our district nurse saw to the wound dressings and finally the stitches removal.

Below our Stendaal house on the hillside were several one-bed homes, mostly for sheltered accommodation. One though was allocated to the district nurse. She offered to adopt a Caddy lamb as per a radio request from Charlie Hunter of Vassa. The kids were all fascinated and petted it through the fencing wire, though it really only had time for the nurse. The little patch of grass that formed her drying green proved limiting, and as it grew it soon developed escape skills. So, back to the park pasture to gambol with the other lambs. Whenever the nurse's car came by, the Caddy would run to greet her. That lasted for a wee while till one day Mavis, Charlie's daughter, came by with a juicy leg of lamb!

Changes were afoot in the bus world with a re-branding of Georgeson and Moore. New partners formed a new company and drivers from the south were recruited. Erik was told his services were no longer required. This made a difficult situation as I obviously required full use of the car. With the kids seen off to school, Erik drove me to the salon, then for Leasks, he would do an airport run, joining me later, it was the return trip home.

An obvious overlap with school we overcame by leaving the back door unlocked, giving the kids access to the utility room. The inside door was locked and it became a little haven for Erika and Darren. Crisps and juice were available, bean bags to relax on plus a little black and white Sony portable TV.

Around this time, we had already begun to research the possibility of selling off the land in the lane that was extant on the Deeds for 5/7. Outline planning had been obtained and we put it on the market. The hope was that with the proceeds we might find a property in Nesting to renovate, or even build on. The narrow lane was deemed, by some, to be incapable of having room for even a caravan—despite the architect's drawings and permissions!

In retrospect, perhaps it was fortuitous, as we really needed to be in Lerwick. Therefore, it made sense for us to develop the lane site if at all possible. We were spurred on as a result of our situation to seek a council house exchange, and advertised for the same in the *Times.* Again, fortuitous it was, that a couple of Nesting origins were of the same mind. So with the council's blessing and assistance, a swap was done.

Chapter 10

It was quite a wrench to leave Nesting, especially as I, a city girl, had really taken to the rural lifestyle. To leave also the friends we made, our nice neighbours too, in that quite short time of seventeen months. The kids were now attending Bell's Brae school, again with new friendships to foster. As far as my work was concerned, it was a Godsend so much more convenient. We pressed on with thoughts of developing our lane 'Kale yards and Stack steids,' as our 5/7 Deeds affirmed. My near neighbour across from the salon, Neil Roger, kindly drew up detailed plans for full permissions. Those were soon granted, so now we would, hopefully, prove the Nay-sayers wrong! But all that would be at a later date. Meantime, it was work as usual, with Erik working for Leasks.

Pushkin didn't take to the move without her acting loopy, her behaviour ever strange as usual. One day of howling gales and rain, the kids came home from school, the door flew open and suddenly a cat flew past them. I tried to catch it but it disappeared behind the washing machine. There was no possibility of enticing it from its lair as it hissed and scratched at any attempt to reach it. I gave up, left food and water, and later we all went to bed as usual. More grub was devoured the next morning and with doors left ajar, it departed No 28 as fast as it had arrived! Whether it was a house stray or a feral hill cat, we never did establish, for we never saw it again. I was pleased to have fed it on such a night.

Our across-the-fence neighbour stopped speaking or acknowledging our family, for what reason we knew not. Eventually, it became apparent that her home was now a Budgie-free zone, and our daft cat was the assumed culprit. That we doubted as Pushkin preferred open spaces and was shy of all humans other than us!

Our big family adventure that summer was our first Continental holiday. It was always our intention to take the kids to other countries, meet other people, and observe their lifestyles. Our target was the South of France. We had to follow quite a convoluted process of travel due to financial constraints. Overnight with P+0.to Aberdeen, kill a day there, then the BR Sleeper to King's Cross. We then had to connect with a coach for onward travel, via a cross-channel ferry to France. Then an all-day and evening journey from the North Coast to the south. French national holidays didn't help our progress one bit, and it was almost midnight before we arrived at our destination Cap d'Agde. Once in our apartment, we all just flopped!

The kids discovered a new toy comprising a plastic tube that one dipped in a little tub of coloured goo. By gently blowing, a massive bubble could be formed, its surface covered in ever-swirling rainbow colours. We purchased some to take home. Upon our return to Shetland, it was a non-event, as the goo in the northern climes had the consistency of well-chewed bubble gum, and refused any attempt at bubble-making!

As well as catching a tan and swimming in the warm sea, visiting the old town was nice and such a contrast to the massive resort. A little Mediterranean boat trip was enjoyable, including a close look at a notorious island prison, but for us more memorable was that as we set sail we observed a young couple at the channel side. They were wrapped around in a large sarong and engaged in heavy snogging. On our return later, two hours, they were still at it in the same spot! Amazing, what you remember.

Back home, there were some quite steep braes in the Norstane/Burnside area, popular with daredevil young cyclists, of whom Darren was one. Throughout his childhood, he developed a knack for bruising himself on hard immovable objects, most often in his quest for speed! One brae proved his undoing, for he performed the classic over-the-handlebars routine. Not only was he badly bruised and grazed, but he'd loosened his front teeth also. He was exceedingly lucky as quite recently, a little local lad had not survived a similar incident.

In the lane, Erik had made a start at soil removal, but a bruised disc put a stop to that. One of my clients took in lodgers, usually building trade chaps, and I enquired if any of them might be interested in clearing the site. They were only too happy to oblige and organised everything. A tiny Kobuto digger did the digging; two little dumpers carted the soil up to the Hillhead and into the shovel of a JCB. The big digger then emptied its cargo into a waiting lorry. Not only did they clear the whole site of earth over three evenings and get paid, but they sold on the loamy black topsoil all around Lerwick. Erik was so relieved and said it would have taken him three years by himself! It would be some time before any building would begin, so in the meantime, the usual workday living went on with the normal round of birthdays and other family events.

After a happy festive season, early 1982 saw us being invited to become hosts for Up-Helly-Aa in the Grand Hotel. I was rather apprehensive not knowing quite what was expected of us Erik assured me it was an honour to be asked, and that no one would be at all critical. So, as a family, we attended after the burning. We had to put up money beforehand and makeup sandwiches etc. None of our invited guests were expected to pay—for indeed guests they were.

The men folk acted as stewards, marshalling the guizers in the corridors and hall, while we ladies catered in the dining area. We all had a roster to adhere to, off-duty time meaning you could enjoy the stunts and sketches that the guizers would perform. Your guests you would ensure had a dram or two throughout the long night. A long night it most certainly was! If you were lucky, you might see your bed by 9 am. I was to find out that, after wilting post-midnight, I found a second wind.

Erik and I went on to host Up-Helly-Aa's for quite a few years thereafter. Our co-hosts were a happy band, and when the Grand's ballroom changed to a disco club, we all flitted to the shiny new Clickimin Leisure Centre.

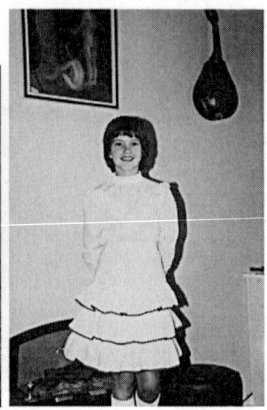

Party girl, Erika (Photo: Erik Young)

Chapter 11

Our next family holiday destination was Vrsar, Jugoslavia. The involved trip south was as previous, but thankfully we flew direct from Gatwick. Interestingly, there are few actual beaches on the rocky coastline, but the foreshore is concreted level with crazy paving, also many dive boards—ideal for this swimming family. More so for Darren who spent so much time snorkelling he was only tanned on his back!

It wasn't always lazing around Istrian shores; we toured some wonderful locations. Postonja caves, Lake Bled, the Lippanzer Stallions (awesome), but best of all was a day trip across the Adriatic to Venice. Our little (Earl-sized) ship gave us a return evening sailing from near St Marks Square, with a golden setting sun reflecting hazily across the glistening lagoon.

There were many interesting aspects of life in Tito's country; exchange rates were fixed daily across the nation, as were fuel prices. We were glad we were on a half-board tariff as shopping could be a nightmare. The kids were gasping one day downtown for juice. Erik said to make it Coca-Cola as at least it was a global brand, and we entered their equivalent of a supermarket...No! You had to place your order at one counter and get a slip. This you took to the payment counter and paid. Your validated (rubber-stamped) slip you took to the serving counter, and when called forward, a shop assistant would serve you according to the details on your surrendered slip. What a palaver! Equally bizarre were the smelly toilets. They were overseen by little old ladies, usually knitting, who held their hands out for small pennies, then handed you two sheets of toilet paper!

During the high holiday season, everyone seemed to have employment. Pretty students, on vacation, did points duty in town intersections, resplendent in pristine white military-style uniforms. Our regular waiter in the evenings had a bit of English and told us that though the holiday work is only part-year, they received a weekly wage all year. Off-season, they were back in their villages helping around the family smallholdings. No such thing as Dole Simples!

We all soon fell in love with Jugoslavia, visiting many times as prices were so reasonable. Sadly, all this would disappear with the war. Sad indeed for the people of this region with its multiple ethnicities.

Joining us soon after our holiday was our ever-keen joiner from Edinburgh. He had got word of our intentions with the land in the lane and expressed his wish to be involved. Here was a chance to be employed in house construction, interpreting architect's drawings, and ground up, in fact, every aspect of the building trade. His terms were as before with 5/7, and in August, the laying of the footings (foundations) on the plot began. Erik had again purchased a small truck for the duration, and many a cargo did it carry, but being a flatbed with sides, a lot of shovel work was required! Bus driving became part-time and ad hoc, to facilitate Erik's part in the build. Having the drop-down settee at the salon, upstairs, meant private accommodation for the builder. He would cycle to and from Norstane to join us for the family meal of the day at teatime (dinner). His breakfast he made himself at the salon and around midday, he and Erik ate packed lunches that I had prepared.

The only interruptions to the building work were, of course, Sundays, also festive breaks with his return to the city. Local family excursions and sea-angling made up for diversions, also serious cycling—his exercise, and hobby. Up-Helly-Aa was a new experience for him, plus a family wedding in April. My brother-in-law Victor and Elaine got hitched, with Erika as the Bride's Maid. A great night was had at Chapel House, with good grub and the lively resident band.

Our builder indicated to us with some notice that as with 5/7, he would appreciate no distractions in his construction of the staircase, dog-legged this time. As the time grew near, Erik realised it would be smack in the middle of the school holidays. He purchased a tent for us two, the kids each having a pup tent. Loading up his Thulecraft dinghy with supplies and camping equipment, the menfolk towed it to Elvis Voe, North Bressay.

On the beach, they found a pallet which they hauled up onto the bank. Everything was placed on it, the dinghy upended and placed on top. All was made secure, and then they returned to the harbour.

A few days passed before the salon was due to close for annual holidays. Come the Saturday afternoon, the family set off aboard Erik's boat 'Windward.' The weather was really kind to us as we set up camp. "Fish for tea," said Erik, and he and Darren set off on the short journey round to the score. They were no time away before they returned with their catch three Haddock and a small Whiting. You can imagine their disappointment when I informed them the one thing I forgot was potatoes! "Haddock 'n' beans, now that's a first," mumbled my hubby.

We really couldn't have been more lucky with the weather. A large Scandinavian high extended to cover the Isles—I was told! Across the two weekends of our stay, we never once had rain. I still hadn't gotten used to the extended daylight hours in Shetland, so it was a sleeping bag up over my head. Nighttime was peace itself, if only the night could have been longer the dawn chorus is very early thereabouts. The gulls I had become inured to, but avian visitors to our tent we could have done without. Chattering conversations, twittering birdsong, and the flapping of tiny wings on canvas. Up under the fly sheet they came, to sit on the inner tent ridge—inches from our 'sleeping' faces! Our food containers became an attraction for 'Forkie Tail,' or Earwigs as I know them. Ah! the joys of the great outdoors.

I really shouldn't carp, for as the holiday went on, the weather just got better and better, plus the temperature continued to rise. By the second weekend, it topped 70 F, sufficient at one point to give Hubby a touch of sunstroke. He had to take to the tent and have a lie-down. But we wandered the area, climbed up to the big gun, explored Aith's Voe by boat and the highlight—a trip round to Noss.

We trekked up the south side of the Isle to the Noup. A packed lunch with juice was enjoyed by the cliff edge, to the sight and sounds of thousands of sea birds. Our return to our little ship was across the moorland occupied by Bonxies, who took ill with our trespass and dive-bombed us. The nest areas were devoid of young, now on the wing.

Upon reaching our moored boat, we found that the rock our captain had secured it to be now submerged. With the sky reflecting on the shiny sea, it was impossible to see it. "I'll have to wade out to catch the rope by the bow, and then back along to the rock," Erik said. He was rather miffed for he had used a rock that was above the line of tangles on the beach. Anyway, he stripped right off and we all asked, "Everything?" He said that with no towel, his drawers he would use to dry off. Not another human was to be seen in this secluded and wild space, so into the cold sea, he waded. He retrieved the bow rope and made his way to the rock, at which point, an engine was heard just over the sound on Bressay. Over the hill rolled a Leask's coach, disgorging its cargo of binocular-wielding birdwatchers! A sense of urgency suddenly overtook Erik's endeavours as he floundered ashore to pull in 'Windward.'

Our quiet little bay and encampment became rather busy that second weekend as a Yacht overnighted, and we had visitors by sea for Sunday tea—the not-long-married Vic and Elaine. It was salon re-opening for business on Monday, so it was back to the harbour and home. All in all, a wonderful staycation.

A hard week followed playing catch-up with my clients, and the usual housework. The lads pressed on with the house building, and once the lovely newly fabricated stairs were installed, it was plaster boarding time. I was really impressed with their progress, there having been no extra assistance involved, other than the window frames courtesy of Mr Bolt at Peter Leith's. Also the exterior render, a wet dash, courtesy of R. McDonald an excellent job.

With a hand-built kitchen utilising MFI doors, by our joiner, of course, the property was now just requiring decoration. With the festive approaching, our builder finally returned home. It was then 'all hands' with rollers and emulsion. Being of small stature the messy job of cupboards fell to me!

As a footnote to a very hectic year, I might add that in the midst of the turmoil, in May, I shipped myself off to Forrester Hill Hospital in Aberdeen. Medical advice was that it was time to come off the pill, and while Hubby was ambivalent regarding vasectomy, I nevertheless was advised towards my being operated on for sterilisation.

Foundation for Sell-Build, Reform Lane (Photo: Erik Young)

Summer holiday, Isle of Bressay (Photo: Erik Young)

(Photo: Author's collection)

Chapter 12

Christmas and New Year came and went with our last festive at Norstane, Erik's parents as usual invited us to our seasonal dinners. It was carpet fitting time at our new home, after tiling in the kitchen and bathrooms. So, on the 21 January 1984, we flitted to 'CLOSSBIGGIN.' The name was given by Erik's Uncle Tommy of the Lodberrie. The other name for a lane is Close, pronounced Closs locally, and he added that to the local name for a building—Biggin. Hence CLOSSBIGGIN.

In May, we welcomed my mum and dad, up by steamer to inspect our new home. They had previously been to Shetland in '74 when we were still in Scalloway. They also came on a P and O Minicruise, late summer '79. My mum was especially pleased to check out my salon down the lane and of course her grandchildren. It was good to see Mum even though she, at times, seemed a bit distant.

Still paying off due monies to Hay and Co. for our self-build, cash was tight in regard to a holiday. Erik got a cheap car from Larry Sutherland's garage. A cheap roof rack was attached, Hubby having made a plywood box for the same. We stuffed the car with all our camping gear and boarded the 'Blue Canoe' for Aberdeen. Heading south, a stopover in Edinburgh gave the kids a chance to catch up with their cousins. In fact, in just about every trip Erik made it a point to always visit Edinburgh, either on the way or on return.

We booked a pitch at 'Greenacres,' County Durham, a lovely area. More especially, it was no great distance from my aunt and uncle, the Bowers, at Haltwhistle. They were absolutely delighted to see me, and my family. Durham City is beautiful, and among other excursions, we had a wonderful day out at the Living Museum of Beamish.

Not long before Christmas, Clossbiggin became home for another resident – Baggy. One day, as the kids were setting off for their schools, a few minutes later, the door opened and they shouted in that a kitten was following them. It darted past them and myself and into our kitchen/diner. He was very hungry, polishing off Pushkin's plate, and then licking his lips he made straight for her litter tray behind the door.

I took him to the police station nearby, assuming by his actions and that being house-trained, he must belong to somebody. Two days later, I got a phone call about the little black cat. The sergeant begged us to take him in as he had exhausted their allocation of dog food! Also, the only response to a local radio appeal was from a chap who, though having a heart of gold was rather fond of alcoholic beverages. At times, he couldn't really look after himself, let alone a cat. I couldn't let that happen and so he came to stay.

Pushkin was not at all happy with this interloper, in fact, her behaviour became so erratic and destructive that we took her to the vet. With her age and evil antics, he felt it best to agree that we had given her a good life. It was distressing all around, especially for Erika and Darren. We would go on to find out that in fact, Baggy was no kitten. A Locum at Edwin Moar's surgery said that he was approximately one year old!

He said he could tell because of the Testicle size. We were not convinced as he was so small. Erik said that Baggy was simply a 'gifted' kitten!

He was certainly gifted in his nature, loving everybody and so placid. The only time he got excited was when I was cooking fish. He would cry at the window, or if he was aware of a passer-by in the lane, he would cry at the main door and was usually let in to become a pest to me. I was forever thinking him so friendly that he might be carried off. He would follow Erik down Reform Lane when heading to Conochies for a paper. He would stop at the bottom and cry, so Hubby popped him in his jacket. The shop assistant would get a fright to see two green eyes staring out!

At Christmas, we welcomed Erik's parents to our very first festive dinner in our own home. It took me some time to realise that it was our own home no more rent. Baggy took to Sonny immediately, forever perched upon his chest!

One bonus of our new location was the proximity to Shetland's only Chinese restaurant. The Ma family were very friendly and we as usual were invited to quite a few of their parties. The tables would be re-arranged, end to end, and what feasts they had. Every now and then Sai Chun would command two cooks back to the kitchen, who would reappear bearing trays of yet more yummies!

At various times. Erika and Darren made good pocket money there. Erika was usually at the takeaway counter, while Darren was up to his elbows in the sinks as a dishwasher.

When we first looked hard at our 5/7 Deeds, it was apparent that the gas bottles supplying the restaurant kitchens were, in fact, on our land. A local lawyer, after some considerable time, finally concurred that the land did indeed belong to us. It transpired that the previous owner had informed the Ma's that the plot was her drying green. There was, until we cleared the site, a pole or two extant thereon. We had no wish to relinquish ownership and instead leased the area to the Golden Coach for a Peppercorn rent.

Erik would brook no sitting around and come Sundays it was time to explore. To the usual protestations, we would set off in the old Vauxhall to various destinations. Hiking cliffs, or ascend high hills, all in the clean fresh air of these beautiful islands. Finances remained tight, so no holidays away were on the cards. However, it became an opportunity to invite the kid's cousins up to experience a Shetland summer in '85.

We invited the two eldest from my sister's families, Roy and Maxine, purchasing flight tickets on their behalf. With mostly lovely weather, we toured extensively, including Mousa, Tingwall Museum, Town Hall tower, Eshaness, but best of all a glorious day sunning and swimming at Minn beach. At one point, Maxine asked about having a Pee. We all said, "Didn't you go in the sea?" With the answer in the negative, Erik directed her to the south side of the Ayre, under the overhanging bank. Upon her return, I asked, "All OK?" To which she replied, "No, a seal was watching me!" Very quiet on the home journey, and no doubt in some discomfort, she declared, "I think every beach should have a public toilet!"

With the relatives away, having hopefully had an experience to remember, it was back to the rigours of hair care and normality. August saw me join Hubby and Darren at the 'Eela' (sea-angling), but only because it was mirror calm. As it turned out, such conditions were not conducive to Piscatorial hook-munching!

In the autumn, Darren took up a new sport Kung Fu. An employee at the Golden Coach, Lewey Ho, was apparently well-versed in this Oriental discipline. Joining him at Clickimin Centre was his neighbour, Jamie Pepper. A waiter whispered to Hubby that Lewey was in fact a Si Fiu, and back in Hong Kong such persons might be contracted to 'Do a number' on someone who had wronged them! To us, he was just a nice family guy.

Occasionally, a major supplier of hair products might hold a seminar, usually over a weekend. I took advantage of one such in October as it was held in Edinburgh, giving me a chance to visit family. Erik, Erika and Darren accompanied me; my tax-deductible expenses made a dent in the travel costs. Hubby and I did the hotel thing, the kids sleeping- over with their cousins. Great to see them all as, other than Roy and Maxine's visit, it had been sixteen months since we last connected.

As 1986 approached, it heralded a big change in regard to our hosting duties for Up-Helly-Aa. As previously mentioned, the function suite at the Grand Hotel (our festival venue) was to be transformed into a nightclub. Our group approached the manager of the Clickimin Leisure Centre, who agreed that we might hire the function room on a trial basis. Any fears, on either side, were soon allayed with a great night all around as usual. Much as everyone had great affection for the Grand, it was a much smoother operation not having to contend with the crowded stairs and corridors of the old venue.

Summer saw a big event at Shetland's main airport. Fifty years of operation at Sumburgh were celebrated with an air show, with many historic aeroplanes, including a De Havilland Rapide, one of the earliest commercially operated planes to the islands, I was informed. The males enjoyed it immensely, but I was only really interested in travelling in them! Indeed, soon after I would be flying, but from Gatwick, in July, to Primosten in Jugoslavia. It was time for a decent holiday at last, and the Istrian coast didn't disappoint. We all had a wonderful time by the shores, with any exploration using local bus services, Split was a nice place having an ancient palace, but like Lerwick's Fort mostly hidden by houses.

Living in the Lanes was really convenient, but while Clossbiggin was my 'dream' home, its surroundings were more akin to a bomb site. Hubby continued to drive the buses ad hoc, to facilitate his work to clear and redevelop the adjoining areas adjacent to our house. Soon after moving in, he purchased a trailer to attach to the ancient Vauxhall, and once in residence began removing topsoil. Any stones, he kept, if only to lighten his barrow load up the lane. They came in handy later.

In fact, by now we had a fully functioning patio/courtyard at the top end of the house with a block wall to the lane. This Erik dressed, on the lane side, with rubble and stones from the site clearance. A young Bressay schoolboy making his way to the ferry from Bell's Brae often stopped to check on progress. Enquiring just how long this dyke building would take; he was unimpressed, Magnus Wills declaring, "I'm going to call this the Great Wall of Erik!"

I cut the cord in October when Erika, accompanied by her schoolmate Eileen Mustard, set off to Edinburgh for the midterm break. I found it a bit strange, as we did everything as a family and now, an empty bedroom. Anyway, they were staying with my relatives, so no need to worry!

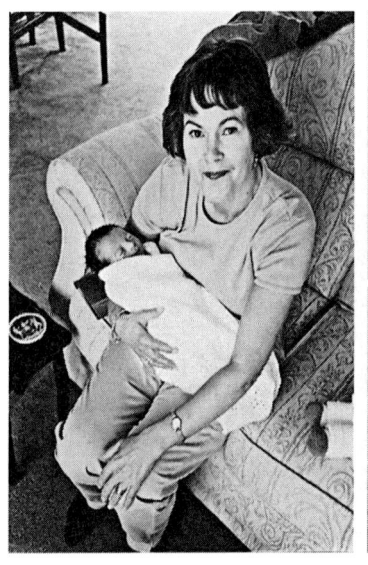

Clossbiggin

Great Wall of Erik (Photo: Erik Young)

Chapter 13

Up-Helly-Aa 1987 saw Darren being invited by a classmate to be a Viking in the Junior Fire Festival, his pal being voted to be the Junior Guizer Jarl. I think he was immensely chuffed and appeared to enjoy every minute of it. Being busy in the salon, I unfortunately didn't see him during daylight hours, but Hubby took lots of photos. However, seeing him march with his flaming torch alongside the little Galley that, within the hour, would be burned to ashes was really something. Not only was he involved with the junior, but also the senior event. Of course, not carrying a torch with all the men, but as a 'Fiddle-box-carrier' throughout the long night. At some point, we would meet up when his Pop-Pop's squad arrived at the Clickimin. Erika assisted me whenever I was on hosting duties in the cafe—Erik, stewarding and MCing.

April brought an unexpected event; my mum decided she must visit. Word had reached her that Loganair was now operating a direct Edinburgh Shetland flight to Tingwall airstrip. Her previous visit, being a weekend mini cruise, meant she hadn't quite got the full measure of my whole circumstance. She was relieved to wobble across to us waiting at the fence gate, (Wot! No security?)…changed days! She was quite happy sitting in the salon watching me at work, and spending time with us in our home. The usual car excursions added to her experience, and while she seemed lucid and engaging, word from Edinburgh was that such wasn't always the case. Also, while she said she'd never set foot in a small plane again, she nonetheless boarded her return flight but appeared somewhat subdued.

Holidays came with the schools' summer break, and once more, we headed for Koversada (Vrsar) Jugoslavia. Another round of sunning, swimming, with Darren and his dad forever snorkelling. The usual excursions, mostly inland, made us love Jugoslavia all the more.

With the schools back, but not for Erika, I had to get used to an empty bedroom once again. College was now the norm for her, at Telford in Edinburgh. Knowing she had quick access to her relatives assuaged any motherly worries.

On the subject of mothers, Erik's mum was increasingly taking to her bed, though to us she only appeared to be losing weight. Apparently, the Rheumatic fever she suffered as a young teen was now haunting her, in that the childhood illness was known to damage the heart. On any nice Sunday, we would entice her, and Sonny, out for a car run. The promise of Shetland's renowned Sunday teas proved irresistible. A different village hall each time, all tended by the local ladies who made up sandwiches and baked all the cakes nothing bought in a delight.

And so the endless toil of work, housework etc., rumbled on. Don't get me wrong, having chosen my own career path, there are no regrets on my part. The constant stream of heads to tend still gave me the satisfaction of knowing that doing my best was, I assumed, appreciated by my clients. They did keep coming back!

As 1988 came and went, two events were to be noted. A short break to Edinburgh gave me a chance to catch up with family. Also, a chance to take my mum in the car to Haltwhistle for a reunion with her sister, my Auntie Justine, and Uncle Noel. I think it brightened her demeanour, temporarily at least, as after treatment she would never again be the mum the family knew.

The Anderson High School summer trip, led by Stuart Hay, Darren joined for travel through several Baltic States, and with the obvious highlight Moscow. He really enjoyed it, though stating he was quite happy to be living in the west!

Erik's sister Peggy arrived from Canada with her little twins for a Shetland holiday, staying at Stout's Court with her parents. When we could, we got them out and about, including the Walls show of '89.

The latest fad Darren had taken up meantime was skateboarding. A Sunday morning empty swimming pool car park, proved handy for him. Another empty bedroom loomed with his departure for college, like his sister in Edinburgh, but at Napier Polytechnic. It wasn't a success. He had chosen an engineering course, but it was all paperwork, only one term having hands-on grease under the fingernails experience. We didn't feel any disappointment, as he was clearly unhappy.

As an interim measure, he was taken on at the Gilbert Bain Hospital as a porter. He was really enjoying his work, even though at one point, he had to experience the 'New Kid' frightener. Late, in the quiet of the night, he was instructed to transport, via the lift, a corpse down to the morgue. Humming gently to himself, he was astonished when the lifeless body passed wind! He couldn't get out of the lift fast enough.

Apparently, it was some sort of initiation dealt out to new employees with typical NHS black humour.

Being home meant he wouldn't miss out on his first year in the big Up-Helly-Aa, carrying a torch alongside his granddad in the procession of 1990. Later that year, a trip to the capital was mainly to see Mum who was receiving treatment in the Royal Edinburgh Hospital, her mental state showing little sign of improvement. There was also no improvement in Erik's mum's health either, as twice she had been to Aberdeen Royal Infirmary for heartwork, but wouldn't sign the obligatory forms. Sadly, she passed away in December. Peggy arrived yet again from her home in Canada but for no holiday. After the funeral, she stayed on over the festive, taking Beth's place at our Christmas dinner table. Also being company for her dad and hosting the Ne'erday dinner for us at Stout's Court.

The spring of '91 saw Erika entering the property market. Financial institutions were falling over themselves for business and were offering 100% mortgages. We stood as guarantors, but we had no qualms as we had observed just how astute she was monetarily. Plus, she had been stung in the past, with flat-sharing in her student days. During this time, Darren passed his motorcycle test and was well chuffed having passed the first time. He quickly moved up in engine size from his 100cc learner bike.

Summer and Erika arrived home having finished college, but in no fit state to commence employment. She had fallen foul of Shingles, so it was time to recuperate. Recuperating was what I had to do come January '92, with a trip to ARI, Aberdeen for a hysterectomy. I was so happy that Erika returned home to care for me. Not only that, she accompanied

Hubby to Clickimin at Up-Helly-Aa to stand in for me at the hosting.

Darren meantime had been accepted for basic training in the Royal Navy, and for the past few months had done some serious training of his own. This surprised me, but he set his mind to it, and all we could do was offer encouragement. Off he went to Torpoint in Devon and to HMS Raleigh. Having completed the BT we, as parents, were invited to his Passing Out Parade. In April '92 at Torpoint, Erik and I watched as the various divisions (Darren's was Fisgard), marched the parade ground in blazing sunshine to a military band, recognising the rear admiral attending, then leaving the tarmac to fling their cheesecutters high in the air. How Darren found his again wouldn't prove a problem as, like his father, he is rather large in hat size!

As an engineer artificer, he would attend HMS Sultan in Gosport, adjacent to the Naval docks in Portsmouth. Here, we were invited to yet another Parent's Day in June. Quite a trek for us not like the walking distance of Anderson High! But, most enjoyable, and of course the usual Edinburgh stop off.

Again, we headed south, as come September, it was 'Key of the door' for Erika. We were happy to acquiesce to her requests so, with Darren up to the 'Smoke' from Gosport, in London we attended a performance of Carmen Jones. Special! Erika then returned to Edinburgh with us two in tow, and a meal was had at The Witchery by the castle. Again, special! Her flat was pinned for the cutting of the birthday cake, with her many cousins and relations attending the party.

Concern was growing within my family in regard to my mum. Erika had reported behaviour similar to Parkinsons, but one of my sisters had researched her medication and it was a side effect of the heavy dosage prescribed. It began to look as though 24/7 care might be an option, but in the meantime, my sisters visited regularly at 91 Redford Road. Mum's demeanour while mostly distant, always brightened when shown attention from the family dog. A while back, my sister, Shirley (The animal lover), had been asked to take on a friend's dog. The girl had become a single mum, and what with three little girls to contend with, a lively young dog in the mix was more than she could handle. Being introduced to the dog, Mum took to it right away, so adoption was swift – Shirley already had a menagerie! A sandy-coloured Whippet cross, it was ideal as she had the most placid nature; even cats sensed it and would sidle up for a 'Hello' sniff! Mum christened her Sasha.

A Fad of the early 60s witnessed on the shores of Southern France was the use of a bib-like device adorning the chests of bikini-clad beauties tanning in the Mediterranean sun. Its upper surface was mirror-like, reflecting the sun's rays up under the chin of the wearer, to stop any chance of untanned white rings appearing! This obviously resonated with Mum, as she was often observed on any sunny day, sitting by the door of No 91, Sasha at her feet, holding a tea tray covered in Bacofoil up under her chin!

Darren at HMS Raleigh (Photo: Erik Young)

All together at Clossbiggin (Photo: Erik Young)

With Erik's parents (Photo: Erik Young)

Chapter 14

On the home front, we decided that, due to staffing problems, we should sell 5/7. It wasn't an easy decision, and when it went to a dentist, it was quite a wrench. I had previously approached Harry Jamieson of 'Harry's' to enquire about renting a chair in his disused barbershop. This idea met with his approval, and I was immediately set up with a chair over a weekend. Clients moved with me so no problems on that score. With no rates, no building maintenance, no insurance and no wages; it was the best thing I could have done.

Erik's dad had been failing through '92 as having twice had treatment for prostate cancer, he now was struggling. We decided that, since he wouldn't move in with us, we should move into Stout's Court. Clossbiggin had been mothballed meantime and we refurbished Beth's bedroom to our requirements. It became obvious to us with both offspring flown the nest, that Clossbiggin was now rather surplus in our situation. Sonny had for many years entreated the council to provide him with a porch—to match those already a feature in the area. Many a time, we would visit to find him, feet in the fire, with snowflakes blowing in around the patio door and landing on his head! He said that we should proceed with 'Right to buy' in his name.

So Clossbiggin was put on the market, and we did indeed pay for 2 Stout's Court. Our time in Reform Lane came to an end in September '92, when we said goodbye to our self-build. An even bigger wrench this time, considering the work and effort that went into its creation.

Looking after Sonny was quite demanding, but it had its lighter moments also. One night, we were awakened to find him out of bed, and appearing very concerned. About what—we knew not. He demanded to know if there was enough food. We asked why, and he stated it was for all these people! The diamorphine was obviously shaping his thoughts. Another time, he was attempting to put his dentures in the fire. A big crash in the night brought us from our slumbers to find him all tangled up in that which had been airing on the muckle clothes horse. Beth's walking stick he had taken to using for exercise whenever he felt stiff. This, we found him with, trying to catch fish in the stove.

A retired janitor responsible for school furnaces, he brooked no interference with the stove his stove. Such, that when he'd passed on, his apparition might appear between the inner hall and the living room doors should we dare stoke his fire! When we first moved in, and trying to help him, I thought to tidy up his collection of old trainers which encompassed the hearth all around the stove. There was little chance of his ever using them, but even with holes in the soles, he did not wish to part with them. It was common knowledge he never bought a pair but would visit Charlie Summers at the high school to check out the lost property. He would usually select a 12-year-old pair since he had tiny feet.

Well, the situation, and we knew it, wouldn't last. On 17 May 1993, Sonny passed away. Again this prompted a

Canadian visitor, Erik's sister Peg. The funeral was very well attended for one his age, and the Big Kirk emptied to the strains of 'The Norseman's Home' his request recognising his being an ex-jarl. After all formalities, Erik insisted on a complete break. Off we set on the ferry to 'Do' the North of Scotland by car. The weight of care lifted from us both, but I think especially for Hubby, as he had latterly given up any work to be with his dad all day, every day. We also took a trip soon after to Edinburgh to visit my mum, who unfortunately was now resident in a care home in Churchhill. During these trips, we employed designers to revamp Stout's Court, it having passed to us on Sonny's death.

No sooner were we back from the Edinburgh trip, than it was almost an about-turn. Mum had passed away in August—suddenly, but peacefully. So it was back aboard the St Clair, yet again. Once again, for a family get-together, but in much less happy circumstances.

At Harry's, I was joined by Elaine Fraser and we got on very well together, she also rented her own chair. As well as my existing clientele, the 'HARRY'S BARBER SHOP' sign was very apparent to any visiting shipping, and Fisher lads and the like were always appearing. A quick gent's cut was easy money, and we both benefited thereby. Harry himself still used the laundry facilities for football kit—he managed the Junior Spurs team. Many a Monday, I would have to clear the machines of same, folding them up for his collection.

A coin-operated phone he'd installed when I started incoming calls only, other than cash in the slot. 50 pence a call and Elaine was always feeding the box to call friends no mobile phones back then. Harry soon twigged as her calls were brief, and a substantial credit accrued. Often he would traverse, from his garret office, through his big department store to take advantage of any surplus! Harry was such a character, and I was so glad to have known him on a personal level. Even at Christmas time, Elaine and I, and our partners, were invited to his grand staff parties. Apparently, he was well known in toy circles and would attend an annual trade fair in England. Being the good Guizer that he was he would turn up dressed as a schoolboy sucking on a lolly!

September saw us taking the hot Sun at Vera Playa, Almeria, Southern Spain. Relaxing. Oh, the joy!

Our little, transformed flat at Christmas had our expected guests, Erika and Darren. Any joy was dampened by Erika's appearing to be suffering from a debilitating malady. No medic could form a positive opinion of her condition, and so in January 1994, I accompanied her to ARI, Aberdeen. I was not involved in any way with her consultation as she was an adult. That situation remained thereafter however much I, as a mother, was worried and concerned. Hubby and I surmised that for whatever reason, her immunity system was compromised. She had suffered glandular fever as a teen, and we thought that might be a trigger to what could follow.

The big event of January was that Mr Young and I would celebrate 25 years of marriage. I had heard stories from my Auntie Justine of her times and travels in the Far East, Uncle Noel being a captain in the Catering Corp. As the Hong Kong situation would change soon, I thought to visit it, and Hubby agreed, if we might take the second week in Bali—a place he'd always wished to visit. What my aunt didn't tell me was just how cool it could be at that time of year.

Upon our arrival at the Hotel Excelsior, flowers and fizz were waiting for us from the kids, but we chittered in our lovely room. Erik adjusted the overhead heater, cool to warm, to no avail. Transpired it was the air-con! Pyjamas don't figure in our wardrobes, so it was off to purchase lovely Red Silk PJs. At Marks and Spencer, we bought vests for Hubby which extended down to his mid-thigh! We tried to imagine the average Chinaman wearing the same.

Our actual anniversary date was an evening boat trip to Lamma Island for a seafood banquet, with the waves lapping under our feet at the shore-side restaurant. On the return trip to Aberdeen Harbour, we were intercepted by a patrol launch, shining searchlights in our eyes. We were allowed to proceed, us not being involved in any nefarious employ!

Bali was indeed an experience; such beauty all around. But if we saw one temple, we saw heaven knows how many others. I'm sure they are of deep significance to the native population, but oh, dear! Please no more. We travelled many miles to visit and view a sacred (everything was!) volcanic mountain, which proved invisible—like the Bressay Ward on a dreich day. The climax of our stay was to visit the most sacred(!) Temple of Tanna Lott—the one on all the brochures, when we arrived the heavens opened, hosing it down, and the dirt car park looked like a bubbling stew. With only flip-flops and sandals, we refused to leave the bus, despite the desperate entreaties of our guide. Forty minutes we sat there, with a few others similarly attired, and when we drove away, the sun resumed its duty!

One night, we were awakened by a commotion near our room. A hut, and run, held several geese which we assumed were kept for their eggs. These creatures were being harassed by stray dogs, and what with all the barking and squawking, sleep was impossible. I decided to go to reception and reported the situation to the night manager. His response—a shrug. Back in our room, and against Hubby's advice, I shouted out the window at the dogs, to no avail. Giving up, we closed the window/shutters and tried to sleep. The sound of helicopters in my ears (and Hubby's) informed us of night-time invaders—the dreaded Mossies! The next half hour was spent chasing and dispatching them. What carnage! Our room walls were now spattered with our blood, and would have provided thought for an expert in the field of criminal forensics!

All in all, our Far East trip was the most enjoyable and interesting. Back in the UK, a stopover at Erika's Corstorphine flat gave us a chance to meet up with some people we hadn't seen in years. Erika had arranged a 25th anniversary dinner for us at the Hunter's Tryst Pub, just up the road from my childhood haunts. The self-same property that fascinated me when it was a Piggery. The bridal party were all there, plus loads of my relatives. Unfortunately, my mum, having passed away was not present, just like on my wedding day. Darren attended also, travelling up from HMS Sultan, and it was a great night.

Darren's 'Key of the door' fell in April; so up from Gosport he came, and down from Shetland came we. It was only a weekend leave for him, so it was a big family party at Erika's flat. Erika organised all in her usual efficient manner. Summer leave, though, gave him a chance for relaxation at home in Shetland. He was quite impressed with the transformation of his grandparent's old flat. However, I got the feeling that he was keen to get back, if not exactly to the engineering training, but perhaps to another interest entirely!

His detached demeanour probably rubbed off on us too. For a time, we discussed just how many times, and at what expense, we had travelled to and from the Isles. We decided that if we wished to maintain good contact with our offspring, a move to the mainland made sense. These thoughts were reinforced when, previously, my mum had passed away. Attending her funeral had meant yet another P and O trip. With the big Volvo, cabin, plus high-season tariffs, it seemed we were just working to fund the ferry company and air service. I was of the feeling that having spent 23 years on Erik's home territory, getting back to mine would be of benefit to us both, and our children.

Early December, a notice appeared in the public notices of the *Shetland Times*—intimation of my ceasing trading. Two weeks later, I packed up my scissors etc., leaving my colleague Elaine alone at 'Harry's.'

Shetland bikers (Photo: Margaret Fraser)

Hunters' Tryst 25th Anniversary Celebrations (Photo: Author's collection)

Hongkong (Photo: Author's collection)

Chapter 15

Christmas we spent at Erika's, and then house hunting became our main pursuit. A flat, a mere ten-minute walk from the Oxgangs home of my teen years, seemed to suit and we quickly snapped it up. An elderly lady, widow Mrs Forbes, was intent on doing the house viewings herself, declaring everything as perfectly adequate—most of which was as elderly as her good self! In the midst of the usual legal to and fro, she had apparently (against medical advice) made it up to the flat one more time, to clean and switch off the ancient fridge. Upon her return to the Astley Ainslie Hospital where she was an in/out patient, she took to her bed and passed away soon after. On several occasions, while living there, sounds in the night emanated from the single bedroom where latterly she had slept!

Needless to say, all that was 'Perfectly adequate' skipped off to the dump, meaning a lot of work was now required to bring the place up to date. We settled in well, even though I was told I had to take my clothesline down after my 'Day!' Erik sorted that out by stringing all six poles with a new plastic-coated wireline, defying any removal. The situation changed overnight with his, come one, come all approach. First out got the first choice of line, all else wherever.

Top floor living was OK, us being fit, but it didn't last. The mid-flat below us was vacated by its owner, their moving to other accommodation, but not sold. It was let to pay their new mortgage. The tenants, a young couple, were neighbours from Hell. Any request to reduce noise levels was rebuffed. Yelling arguments seemed to be the young Irish girl's way of life. Sunday mornings took on a pattern following the noisy Saturday evening return from clubbing or whatever. "I'm leaving!" she let the neighbourhood know at full volume. I imagined a, behind lace curtains, chorus singing, "Yes, please do!" Her erstwhile lover would follow her down the street, pleading for her return heaven knows why. Occasionally, he would get a phone call from the Irish flight desk at Edinburgh Airport, to come and fetch her.

Ms Ford, a retired teacher, who'd lived there in peace for 30+ years was singled out for particularly evil treatment. Her plant pots in the stairwell upended, hoover left running for hours above her head.

Thankfully for us, we could soon sell on Stout's Court, having had a very good tenant there in the interim. This gave us a way out, and the combined values allowed a move to a detached villa in Currie. This we purchased from a lecturer at Heriot-Watt Uni, just down the road. He was known locally as the Nutty Professor, and there were aspects of the property that chimed with his nickname. The attractive little fireside and mantel in pale cream Marble, he was mortified to see described in the sales brochure as 'composite material.' He said we could employ his cleaner if we should so desire. I bit my lip on that one, as it still had that single male, dusty-musty-casual-disorganised look. Despite the close proximity of the Weaver's Knowe Pub and Lounge, he thought fit to attempt

Home-brew, with mixed results just something else to clear up.

When we moved down from Shetland, other than doing up the Caiystane Gardens flat, I was hoping to take a break from the 'hair.' Erik had expected to 'walk' into a job at Lothian Buses (previously the corporation), but that was not to be. An agreement had been reached among the protagonists in bus routes (We were now in a de-regulated territory), and Lothian had surrendered West Lothian at the first bus exit from Edinburgh's local service, city streets routes. The upshot was that there was no recruiting at Annandale Street for the foreseeable future. Only poorly paid work with Tupenny—ha, penny outfits were available. Certainly not enough to keep the wolf from the door.

So, (Sigh!) looking for a job, I happened upon a salon for sale in Gorgie, near Balgreen Road, it being at a reasonable price. The bank came up with a top-up loan, and we purchased 'Contrasts.' Described as pleasant and attractive decor, my impression was old and tired. Erik named it the Little Shop of Horrors. It came with one stylist, Pamela, who the sellers were keen I should keep on. That made sense as I was the new kid in town, with a stylist having an established clientele, it meant business as usual. I just had to build up my own client list. Luckily, that didn't take long, as the nearest salon was a bit high-class and expensive for the area.

Coincidental with our redecoration of Contrasts, I got word that a salon further in towards Dalry was closing down. I approached the lady who was retiring, as she had Wella bank driers of the type I had used in Shetland. A deal was done, and what a difference they made for my shampoo and set ladies. While I hadn't missed the hairdressing, I quickly got into a rhythm again—it seemed it had all become second nature to me, like riding a bike.

August '95 saw Darren pass out from his Naval training, so with Erika, we took a trip to Hampshire. Quite an experience seeing all the other proud mums and dads at the parade and awards ceremony. Back to Edinburgh, where Darren had expressed a desire to see the military tattoo at the castle. It was our first time, with Darren pointing out certain aspects of service personnel marching drills. A truly wonderful experience, especially when the sun dipped behind the ramparts creating a unique atmosphere.

July '96, and an invitation to a wedding meant a trip back up North to Shetland. It was from our friends and former neighbours Bill and Margaret Fraser, whose son Alistair was to be wed. His intended wished to experience the Isles, and so, after the Big Kirk it was to the Shetland Hotel for a lovely meal, and dancing to the music of the lively band Da Fustra. Lively indeed, as one Macho dancer decided he would Birl me airborne – no chance! I let go of his hands and he slithered across the dance floor on his bottom.

At the post-wedding party on Sunday, at the Fraser's house, I learned that Margaret had also hit the floor during the dancing. She was struggling to be a hostess, as her wrist was in a cast and sling! So all the local ladies present mucked in, though the bride and her mum took to their beds as they were tired(?)—doing very little.

Happily for our situation, Erik had got his (hoped-for) job with Lothian Buses. Always on the lookout, he spied their advert for part-time school bus drivers—even that would make more than what he was earning. At the interview, and with his past employment with the corporation, he was handed a job on the spot. What a relief for Hubby, as he was so frustrated with some of the outfits he'd worked for. Now it was a good wage, plus a local government pension.

Pentland hills (Photo: Erik Young)

Wedding guests, Lerwick (Photo: Margaret Fraser)

Chapter 16

Our Currie home turned out to be the original Wimpey show house in the area, us never realising it had been finished to a better standard than others. This information we gleaned from our new neighbours. More hard work was required, however, to modernise our 1950s-style home. On removing the ghastly stair carpet, I was pleased to see that the Virgin wood concealed was Parana Pine just like the beautiful staircase at Clossbiggin. I determined to refurb, and more usually when Erik was driving evenings, that is indeed what I did. A bit of a marathon, but all agreed it was worth it, especially with a couple of coats of varnish after disposing of several layers of white paint.

Midsummer 1997 saw Erik's sister Peggy on a European Odyssey, hooking up with old friends and colleagues from the past. She stayed over with us for a six-day capital visit. At the weekend, we toured Fife and East Lothian with her by car.

In August, Darren and his girlfriend Jane Pask got engaged and travelled up for a family celebration. A visit to our favourite Chinese restaurant in Dalmeny Street, the Yee Kiang, meant all his cousins could wish them well. Jane was especially pleased to witness the Tattoo, not really having any idea what to expect.

Our holiday that year was to Costa Natura, Estepona, which due to its proximity meant we could visit Gibraltar. What a rock! Hubby was especially impressed with all the tunnels carved from the rock with various gunports all around. Neither of us was at all impressed with those apes though! Estepona we found to be a busy working port. While having beautiful wide tiled and paved Esplanades, it also had its fishing harbour, plus the usual Marinas. Seafood was always available in the many downtown restaurants.

Our next-door neighbour, an elderly Dutch widow, recommended we take the local bus to a Pueblo Blanco (White houses), called Casares. It didn't disappoint, the drive up into the mountains was interesting in itself. For company, we had locals, young students, the middle-aged, and the very elderly. Every bus window was wide, but still stifling as the climb was at times, a crawl. The smells were a combination of perfume, diesel fumes, cigarette smoke, BO, and livestock—that being hens one old crone had crammed in a basket on her lap.

Another granny held an infant who, mercifully, was of a placid, non-needy nature.

Midday arrival at the terminus, and our driver informed us that the next return was 4 pm. Well, that was more than enough time to take in the beautiful, but simple delights of this lovely place. We entered an inn straight off the bus, where old men sat silently, seriously, studying their Dominoes. The silence at times broken only by a loud roar at various points in the game. Those eating were tucking in, big style, what appeared to be delicious food. Delicious it certainly was, and we couldn't resist, being peckish by this time. Mountain Hare I fancied, while Hubby settled for Wild Mountain Goat chops.

What a feast—and not at resort prices. We soon walked off the calories trudging up and down the unevenly paved lanes and narrow streets. Every door and shutter was wide open, and after Siesta, the high-speed Latin voices within echoed from wall to wall. A memorable day out indeed.

Another memorable occasion took place in June '98. The Norton Owners Club of Great Britain held their Annual Rally in Scotland for a change, so it was more convenient for us to participate. Erik had been a member for quite a few years. He owned two Norton Commando bikes, the earliest a 750 cc Fastback, and the last, an ex-police 850 electric start—an innovation in its time. The rally was to be held on the grounds of Blair Castle, at Blair Atholl. We booked a BnB rather than camping, as was my wish, and Hubby concurred.

We set off fully leathered-up with backpacks stuffed with a change of clothes, toiletries, etc. The sun beat down on our departure, but we found the approach to the Forth Road Bridge congested, with a crawl around the Queensferry roundabout. Then the Heavens opened, a stair rod – deluge we were soaked to the 'hide!' Once clear of the bridge and into Fife, it was a steady ride north. We pulled into the log cabin tea rooms at Birnam, our leathers as soggy as the tea-bags in our saucers!

Checking in at our digs, our elderly widow hostess spelt out her conditions of let, while relieving us of our dosh. We looked for some wire hangers for our bike gear and hung the same on the picture rail but above the electric heater. We then set off to hook up with other rally-goers. On our return, our gear was still damp, as our hostess had been in our room and switched off the heater!

We got some Scottish country dancing at the first night's venue, even requesting our own choice occasionally. The next day was the Rally Ride Out. Most enjoyable, though of course, we knew the terrain well, the lovely vista from the Queen's View the obvious highlight. That night we danced(?) to a band from Dundee, the Glebe Street Blues Band. We wondered if the Broons knew they had such wonderful musicians as neighbours. A long lie-in the next day, just catching the breakfast curfew, before bidding our Landlady goodbye. We then set off Southwards for an uneventful and enjoyable ride home on the big 850 cc.

A trip of more serious milage was, in August, a trip to Canada. Erik's sister's youngest was about to be wed. Karen was, like hubby, born in the Shetland Isles. So, along with Erik's younger brother Victor and his wife Elaine, we made the journey west from Glasgow Airport. Peggy crammed us all into every available space in their lovely Edmonton home.

The ceremony was held on the grounds of the majestic MacDonald Hotel, overlooking a river winding between cliffs and bluffs. It was a scorcher, playing havoc with the makeup! An elderly gentleman officiated, after which we repaired indoors to air-conditioned comfort. Later, we travelled to a premises well used to such events. After the sit-down meal, it was off to the lounge for postprandial refreshments. At one point, we were all requested elsewhere, perhaps to sign a guest register, I can't quite recall. Upon our return to the lounge, it was suddenly apparent that our glasses contents were somewhat depleted. One guest, of questionable intelligence, saw fit in our absence to forage all the tables—sampling and tasting as he went!

With the reception room cleared, it was on with the dance—well, a disco. However, Karen had earlier requested that we might have some Scottish Dancing. To that end, hubby made up a cassette tape comprising 2× sets of Boston two step, 2× sets of St Bernard's waltz, and a Circassian Circle. It meant that before I could join in the dance, Erik became temporarily a 'Caller'—issuing instructions to the music. It proved to be a success, thankfully. Then it was back to the disco beat.

After recovering from all the festivities, Peggy's husband Stan organised for us a Rockies tour. Utilising his pickup and Peggy's eldest's people carrier, all stuffed with camping gear, we set off for the mountains. As we were about to enter the national park, the weather took a turn for the worse, leading to Stan declaring we postpone entry till the next day. We booked into a motel in a logging town called Hinton. Vic and Elaine took a single room (all the beds are doubles); Peg, Stan, Erik and I shared a twin room. No sooner was it lights-out than Hubby and Peggy took to travelling down memory lane. "Na, Erik do you mind…?"

"Yea, Peg 'n' do you mind…?" Stan and I endured this for as long as we could, till finally, I heard a plaintive Stan say, "Peggy, Peggy, please go to sleep, Peggy!"

Well, the Rockies didn't disappoint—stupendous. We visited all the usual tourist stops along the way. The first night's camping was close by the Algonquin River, it's rushing waters encouraging swift slumber. However, poor Elaine had a loud cough which at twenty-minute intervals, tended to interrupt our sleep. At the next setting-up of camp, no one was in a hurry to put up their tents. Only when Vic camped did the rest of us do likewise, but at a fair distance from the twenty-minute alarm! In the morning at coffee, we enquired of Stan if he was disturbed in his sleep. "No, not at all," he politely stated with typical Oriental diplomacy.

"You liar!" said Peg. Enquiring with Vic and Elaine regarding the coughing, Elaine said it was going through a bad patch. Vic said it never bothered him since he slept with his 'dead', deaf ear upward!

One morning I set off to the toilet block taking the basin with me for post-breakfast dishwashing. I'm glad I did, as no sooner had I got in and about to start my ablutions when I was invaded by approximately twenty noisy Italian ladies who all proceeded to strip right off. I quickly filled the basin and took refuge in a stall. So that day, all my 'necessary' requirements had to be met in such cramped conditions.

As a biker, Erik was always on the lookout, and at one lay-by/viewpoint, he was amazed at the vintage of some riders on Honda Goldwings. "How do they hold those things up?" He mused especially as none seemed to have subscribed to any slimming club. The penny dropped as when they all set off, they were already feet-up. Apparently, at crawl speed, from the flat foot plates, small wheels lower—requiring no human legs to steady the mount upright. "Whatever next," said Hubby. We really did have a wonderful time, thanks to our delightful hosts. But it was time to get back to Blighty, to heads of hair, and buses to drive.

Norton Rally, Blair Atholl (Photo: Erik Young)

Canadian Wedding (Photo: Author's collection)

Macdonald Hotel, Edmonton (Photo: Author's collection)

(Photo: Erik Young)

Chapter 17

Approaching 1999 was the realisation that Hubby and I had been hitched for 30 years! In January of that year, the family celebrated the occasion by Darren bringing Jane North to Currie. Erika organised a special night out at 'Hadrian's' in the North British Hotel. Wonderful food and wine. Our taxi ride home was to ever-blinding snow. Jane was excited as she, that night, had never experienced the white stuff! Setting off after their stay she was quite trepidatious of the drive. Darren reported from a service area en route that, south of Biggar, it was totally clear.

Springtime brought change to Contrasts with redecoration, the predominant colour being blue. Business was steady, and I had no concerns in that regard.

Into July and another bike ride northwards, this time to Glamis Castle. It was the Strathmore Transport Extravaganza. Quite an event, everything from pushbikes to tractors, motorbikes to old buses and trucks. Not wishing to witness the proceedings sweating in leathers and combinations, we parked at a spot well away from the crowds of parked cars. We changed into shorts and tee-shirts; our gear stowed and attached to the big Norton. With juice, snacks and three-leg camping stools, we headed for the arena. It really was wonderful, a Grampian TV newsreader in the centre, ringmaster style, giving a running commentary with a radio-mic. A cup of hot tea we purchased from a WWII tea wagon, being served by WVS ladies suitably attired.

Upon our return to the commando, we were rather surprised to find it surrounded by many cars, some occupied. Getting changed proved as problematic as Erik's wardrobe moment in our 1983 holiday. Taking turns to shield each other, getting back into our combinations and leathers was no easy task! A steady run south, till I tapped Hubby's shoulder for a leg stretch. We were just above Kircaldy—Mr Young, once mobile was loath to ever stop. Alighting from the bike, we were amazed to see the exhaust pipe/silencers swinging in the breeze! Still connected at the engine end, the rubber/metal fixings at the rear of the bike had failed. A jury rig of Bungee cords got us home. Subsequently, Hubby's moans to a fellow club member elicited the information that the expensive Norton part could be replaced by BMC Mini exhaust system bobbins at a fraction of the cost, and easily available locally.

Darren and Jane had by this time taken up residence together in Gosport. In August, we took a trip south to visit them and their fluffy cat Lucky. Darren was by now long out of the Navy. Upon finishing his training, he responded to the request of Dockyard choice. Rosyth had not long ceased to be a Naval Base, leaving just Devonport (Plymouth) and of course, Portsmouth. With his fiancé living locally, the choice was obvious. A west country placement would entail a 300-mile round-trip commute. He did, of course, expect the new six months of sea-time. After the Balkan conflict, and with a shrunken Armada, the government of the day increased the standard four-month deployment.

With typical MOD contrariness, he was sent a Cablegram and informed that he would be based at Devonport. Not only that, his first voyage would be as Falkland Island's Guardship—ten months away! At the earliest opportunity, Darren and the Royal Navy parted company. Discussing the situation with male clients while still working in Shetland, I learned that during the years of national service, local lads brought up in a maritime environment usually ended up in army khaki or air-force grey!

St Matthew's Court was a pleasant little flat, and while convenient for Jane's employment, Darren had to endure the ghastly commute in and out of Gosport. Anyway, it was lovely to see them again. A day trip together to the Isle of Wight gave us a chance to visit Osbourne House and its lovely gardens, but after the hot, dry summer, there was little greenery—everything parched.

Equally parched was the surrounding terrain near our October holiday destination in Andalusia, at Vera Playa Hotel. A welcome break from business responsibilities—relaxation in the hot sun. Interestingly, close to the town of Vera is Mojacar, a village atop a huge bluff rising up from the surrounding sandy countryside. Taxi driver Tomas was always parked outside reception, and he was our transport to and from. Another magic place, apparently 'discovered' by the Hippies of the 1960s. Every evening the village square filled with locals yarning, the village Bobby moving on anyone who thought that they might park there. There was even a football pitch at the very edge, with the highest mesh fence I'd ever seen. Whether anyone was ever sent to fetch an errant ball, we never did find out!

The excitement of the approaching millennium was soon upon us all if we dared follow the media hype. Well, as it loomed, we wondered just how we all were expected to celebrate it. Erik said, "Let's have a Hogmanay BBQ!"

"Don't be daft," was the usual response, but that is in fact what we did. We were delighted that Darren and Jane (plus two cats) decided to join us, arriving early enough to celebrate Christmas. Also joining us for Hogmanay were my brothers and their partners and Erika. All would 'crash out' on the premises, in the early hours, of the new century.

Hubby had erected a tarpaulin awning should the weather be inclement, but as it transpired the conditions meteorologically proved benign. Erika assisted me in food preparation Erik dispensed drinks. As the minutes ticked away towards the century's end, in the kitchen, pre-cooking took place ready to transfer to the Barbie coals outdoors. Most of the following I only got a flavour of being on cook's duty, but an appreciated success it was.

Fireworks commenced with a huge sky-rocket, lit on the last note of the Windsor chimes from Big Ben. WHOOSH! It shot off into the night, to a spectacular star-burst simultaneous with the very first strike of the hour at full volume on BBC Radio Four! The next ten minutes was a pyrotechnic display culminating in yet another big sky-rocket, which everyone followed all the way up till its burst, eliciting a big cheer from all, including me—at last!

Burgers and sausages and savouries were now sizzling and were soon devoured. The drink flowed in celebration of what felt like just another Hogmanay, really. Near neighbours first footed us providing a real mix of characters. An abiding memory is of entering my kitchen to find a retired police sergeant, nursing a generous measure of Whisky, in deep conversation with a brother's girlfriend, her puffing away on a big spliff! What subject was up for discussion I know not, but Hubby creased up with laughter when I gave him the news.

More memorable than any millennium event was our son Darren getting married. More of that later. In June, we attended yet another Norton Rally, this time more convenient than the previous. It was held at Scotland's Museum of Flight in East Lothian. This time we did camp using Darren's Vango igloo tent. No problems, other than snoring neighbours! A most enjoyable event, all round. Even Di Luca's Rolls Royce Ice cream van(?) made an appearance on Sunday. Also making an appearance Sunday morning was the Burgerman from the Foot of the Walk in Leith. He was always to be seen in the company of Queen Vic, at the entrance to the Kirkgate Shopping Centre. It transpired that the arranged catering had found a more lucrative venue, so the club was left in the lurch. The drawback was of course, that after feasting on burgers on Saturday evening it was burgers again for breakfast! Hubby's 850 had a damaged camshaft, so his 750 was pressed into service.

September arrived and we were off to Sri Lanka for the holidays. The unusual choice was in fact not ours, but that of Darren and Jane. For it was there that they were to be wed. A fascinating holiday it proved to be. I'm not sure if Darren and his father were at all comfortable kitted out in Highland Dress, for it was rather hot. Quite an occasion also with traditionally dressed locals and musicians, all involved in the actual ceremony. Once wed, the groom and the bride mounted a fully dressed elephant for a beach ramble. At one point in the holiday, I suddenly found myself atop one also, in the company of Darren's sister-in-law. Just how it happened I have little knowledge, one minute we were watching it exercise, the next, we were astride it's hairy back. Back on Terra Firma, it was an outstretched palm demanding money!

Hubby had put warnings on us all, even before leaving the UK, not to drink the water. At the poolside, he said, "Stick to the beer, girls." Did we listen? Asking for water, the smiling barmen brought bottled water, but with tops removed. Needless to say, all the ladies of our party came down with severe cramps and dehydration. Not only did we partake of the salt sachets, but I had to get an extremely painful jab in my rear!

Our Erika suffered more than most, and my elephant companion Sarah was near collapse at the airport. Her brother Marc had to almost carry her aboard. I had visions of her passing out, and us all being trapped in Sri Lanka. It took her three weeks to recover, poor girl. I counted myself lucky to have got the medical treatment that I did, the lady doctor only seeming anxious to relieve me of my British magazines!

The gents didn't get off scot-free, as they succumbed to the Delhi-belly. However attractive and tasty the food is, it would appear you pay good money just to suffer.

Darren was keen to give his angler father an Indian Ocean fishing experience, so from a glossy brochure portraying high-speed shiny craft, he booked a trip. Off they headed in a taxi, early morning, to a nearby fishing port.

Here, the craft supplied was an ancient tub, a local inshore vessel crewed by its two owners. With Marc along too, they sailed west over the choppy inshore waves. Turned out it stayed choppy, as there was no deep sea for miles. Darren suddenly had to make for the boat's toilet (bucket, below!), the subsequent stench emanating from the cabin causing Hubby to retch. Soon, father and son were at the rails polluting the ocean! Marc, meantime, who's only maritime experiences were on a Pedallo, was with a rod in hand quite unaffected. Not only that, he caught a big silvery fish a metre long. Great joy for the crew, as it seems it would make a good price back on the quay.

Assuming our hotel was a tourist hotel, we were all rather miffed when a local family held a wedding also. The trouble was they took over rooms and restaurants that we were using, but now we were side-lined. For two days, we never knew where we might be eating next.

Meeting our Rep proved a surprise. Sharon from Shotts was our girl, and very helpful she proved to be, what with all the medical troubles. She informed us that she stayed locally and was married to a native Sri Lankan called Calum. That raised a few eyebrows. One evening, running the gauntlet of pedlars at the gate, we made out for a beach walk. One chap ingratiating himself to us, in the hope of a sale, asked "Do you know Sharon?"

We replied in the affirmative, eliciting the information that, "She married my friend Kaloom!"

Back in the UK, our newly married couple were now living in Portchester at Portobello Grove. Surprisingly to me, all the surrounding streets had names firmly in a Caledonian groove. Also resident there was Sheba, their dog. She was a Dogue De Bordeaux—of the 'Turner and Hooch' type. A lovely-natured beast, and equally slobbery! When, later in the year, I learned of their intention to visit us at the festive, I was more than a little apprehensive. The breed's claws carry the quick well towards the tips requiring care when clipping them.

Well, come Christmas, they all came to stay at 50 Riccarton Avenue indeed across the year-end also. Darren put warnings—on the biddable animal to the effect that my pride and joy-varnished stairs were off limits. One Sunday morning, I crept quietly downstairs to rustle up tea and toast for Hubby and me to partake of in bed. Sheba, I let out the back kitchen door to do her necessary, re-joining me in the kitchen, then through to her bed in the lounge.

Quiet snores from the other bedroom indicated slumbers still, from our guests. I tip-toed up the stairs and handed the tray to Mr Young. I turned to get back into bed, only to witness a honey-brown missile shoot past my shoulder to crash land in the middle of the duvet! I apparently was not the only one to tip-toe in the stairs. Luckily, Hubby lubby held the tray aloft, and level, but let out a loud expletive. This roused the house, and her master appeared to administer his own volley to the clever Sheba.

Glamis Trip (Photo: Erik Young)

Mr. &Mrs Darren Young (Photo: Erik Young)

Chapter 18

Lots of miles were travelled in 2001. The length of the British Isles, literally. From my favourite college trainee, Odette in Shetland came an invitation to her wedding in May. She never forgot, obviously, my telling her that a Whalsay wedding was something I'd never experienced. These occasions, on this Fisher Island off Shetland's East Coast, are renowned. No one night 'do' here—it's a three-nighter! Almost everyone on the island is involved over the course of the celebrations.

So, Hubby and I winged our way northward, hiring a car from Erik's old boss, Peter Leask. A holiday cabin on the island was our base for two nights out of the three. The wedding was really something, Odette looking lovely in her wedding dress, alongside her new husband Leonard. Lots of dances of the traditional were enjoyed on the night. Night two was held at another venue, with Mae and Mackie's rock band—a total riot. They certainly knew how to party!

A month later, it was off to the far south, in fact, Hampshire. This was to meet our first Grandchild, Tegan. It was to her grandad's chagrin that she didn't hang on a little longer in her mum's warm belly. She was born just before midnight on 3 June—minutes away from sharing with

Gramps on the 4th! She was a very contented and placid baby, and it was lovely to see Darren's family.

September and Erika's birthday saw that milestone of three decades. Where did the time go for my peerie lass?

A big change in my circumstances came about in October. My salon neighbours at Gorgie were keen to expand their premises and approached me regarding buying my shop. As, other than Pamela, staffing had proved problematic—I was tempted. The outdoor pursuits guys, while having a large frontage, had limited floor space. It was the opposite of the TARDIS, the curving display windows disguising the fact that the layout was like an orange segment. A deal was done, my paying off Pamela well. Now time for a break.

Off to the Costa Brava for our holidays, but not to any of the obvious destinations. Blanes is not short of beach and esplanade, but it is mercifully less crowded, it being also a working fishing port. Nice to relax in the sun, but what now? Where now? Well, one becomes used to a lifestyle, and I'm never one to be idle. So, thinking back on my rent-a-chair stint at Harry's in Shetland, I was soon looking for a little shop to rent. This I found after quite a search, with some very dubious premises. I couldn't have been more central in Gorgie at No 203, opposite the Scotmid Co-op, right at the pedestrian crossing.

I was now totally in control, being responsible for all aspects of hair care, from shampooing, cutting, setting etc. Cups of tea/coffee and floor-sweeping were, of course, mandatory! I soon had a full appointment book at CAROL'S, with many of my former clients following me there.

November visitors at Currie were Darren and his family. Little Tegan remained as placid of nature as before, and we really appreciated them making the effort to travel so far with a seven-month-old baby.

June 2002, and it just had to be a special birthday as Tegan reached her twelfth month. So off to Southampton Airport we flew, picked up a hire car, and our holiday began. We toured Devon and Cornwall, staying in a Farmhouse BnB, an open window for 'fresh' air always reminding us of our location. Plus of course, the early morning Cockcrow! It was a lovely break, our highlight was the Lost Gardens of Heligan. But we were keen to head East to Portchester and catch up with the birthday girl.

In July, Erik's sister Peg, husband Stan, and their teenage twins planned a Scottish trip. So, after their Shetland stay, we met them at Aberdeen Airport with a hired people carrier. Repaying our Rockies trip meant we could once again visit the beautiful north and west of Scotland. We BnB'd our way around via all the usual tourist spots. We all had a great time, till finally, back to Riccarton Avenue for their city visit.

One afternoon, after work, I filled the tumble drier in the garage and then set off shopping locally. When I returned, it was to find our house surrounded by fire engines! Well, the garage fire was out by that time, and the guys were busy mopping out. Luckily, neighbours had been quick to spot smoke, but flames inside did quite a bit of damage. One neighbour broke in through the garage's main door and wheeled out Erik's two classic Nortons, phew! Hubby had still to come home after a day shift. I phoned Erika who was accompanying the Canadian party uptown, to the effect that they might stay and eat there. The last thing on my mind was preparing food for seven people. However, Peggy insisted that they would be arriving at Currie as arranged. A day to remember and how!

Darren's family headed north to share Christmas with us at No.50. Lovely to catch up on all their news and have them relax in our home. A fine end to a memorable year—in more ways than one!

My stepdad turned 80 in February 2003, giving us the opportunity to have a big family get-together. Interestingly, it fell on myself and daughter Erika to organise it all. 'Tanner's' at Juniper Green was a location handy for most, and given their reputation for good food, it was most enjoyable. Down the years, it became apparent that, given my family history and my own backstory, in regard to familial associations it was always me that would make the effort.

Like any granny, every chance to meet up with Tegan, I took, and March saw our weekend with a Portsmouth Hotel deal. Not even three months later, off we went again, but this time to a different address. Moving down from the Scottish-named streets on the hill, Darren's little family were now in the heart of Portchester, at 10 Queen Mary Road with a busy little shopping centre five minutes walk away and the Historic Portchester Castle a 20-minute stroll. The A27 passes by the centre shops, making for good road connections.

Our brief stopover to check out No 10 was part of our holidays, this time to Monsena, Istria, again near the little town of Rovinj. The quickest way to town was a water taxi, for a few Dinar. Lots of sun, swimming and seafood, with bands playing live nightly on the terrace.

Upon our return, we played host to my cousin Joan Bowers from County Durham. She was the 'sister' I might have known, had the adoption gone ahead. She was not long widowed and was now linked to her mother's side of the family. She would prove to be our last guest as, come July, No 50 was sold.

A ground-floor flat at Redford Road, in the same block as Dad's, became available. We knocked on the door, asked their expectation of price and a deal was done—if they took down the sales sign. Its condition was not that good, but as Hubby keeps saying, I like a project! The accommodation was our first priority, and not knowing just how long the repairs and refurbishment might take, we purchased a one-bed flat nearby at Galolee temporarily. That premises required a fresh bathroom suite but otherwise required only painting and floor coverings.

Sleeping (for that's all we did) at Galolee, meant every minute not at work, could be devoted to No 87. All the hard work was rewarded with a late holiday break in November, in Cyprus. Boy! How we lazed for the seven days. Our year was rounded off with a festive visit to 10 QMR with Darren and his family.

Jane's tummy, we observed at Christmas, wasn't down to too much Xmas pudding, but to something more special. 25 February 2004 and out popped Mia! So, south we trotted yet again to meet the new addition to Darren's family. This time a wee Blondie with dimpled chin and a ready smile, though she was more of a live wire than big sister Tegan had been.

I really couldn't resist, and when I had the opportunity in May, I was off once more to re-acquaint with my newest granddaughter. This time, I was on my own as Erik didn't qualify for any days off at the time. It was lovely holding the new baby in my arms. I had always felt that I would have loved to have had more children. Hubby always said, "No, one of each is plenty!"

It was just three months before we all met up again. Darren's family arrived in August, staying with Erika at her Forrester Park flat. For transport, Hubby hired a VW people carrier, so we could all travel together on days out. A Hopetoun House event was one, and Blair Drummond Safari Park another, but Tegan's favourite was the North Berwick Sea Pond!

We had intended, once resident at No 87, to rent out the Galolee flat. What a disaster that turned out to be. An acquaintance of Erika's going through a separation pending divorce seemed to fit the bill. Thankfully, they (father and part-time son) departed without too much fuss; the only real damage was to the living room carpet. This could not be cleaned as it was stained with spilt model soldier paints. Barely a year old, it had to be replaced. The flat quickly found a buyer.

We grabbed a late holiday in October in Spain, at Benalmadena. The hotel's 'sea view' was a wedge-shaped little balcony, occupancy of two persons, offering a vertical slot glimpse—between other hotels! Still, there were benefits pertaining to our stay, one being a bar deal unknown to us, and not well advertised. As was our wont we, after dining, ordered a bottle of Rioja and two glasses. The barman filled our glasses and then produced yet another bottle! The 2-for-1 deal was in operation.

One night in the lounge, a Lancashire chap was setting up for Karaoke. That put a smile on Erik's face as he required no encouragement in that regard. At one point, our DJ introduced two little girls, perhaps 9 or 10, who would perform a song he was not familiar with. Well! The audience had a collective jaw-drop at the foul language, and Oedipal inference, in a 'song' by Eminem! Word perfect they were, while blithely innocent of their meanings.

Our lovely Christmas day was spent at Erika's flat, us picking up Dad from next door at 91 Redford Road. A tasty meal, as always, Erika had prepared to be shared with her boyfriend and his young laddie also.

Chapter 19

Our Hogmanay 2005 was in deepest Sassenach land as we visited at 10 Queen Mary Road. The midnight chimes we experienced in the local Masonic club, a friend of Darren being a member. Very enjoyable, but not quite the same as that in the land of Loch and Glen! More important from my perspective was seeing my lovely grandchildren. Many times I wished that we were staying nearer.

December 2004 had seen me realise a childhood dream. Near where I lived in my pre-teen and teen years, and up towards Fairmilehead, were lots of lovely Redstone Bungalows. Everyone who owned one seemed to take such pride in them, with the beautiful front gardens that they tended. A dream is what I thought it would always be, but a 'project' came on the market near the year-end.

With monies banked from the Galolee flat and bridging finance till No 87 could be sold, we offered what we could afford. As so often happens in the fraught territory of house buying, ours was not the highest offer, so Hubby and I resigned ourselves to the refusal. Two days later, a phone call came to say that the top price buyer did not in fact have the necessary finance set up—it was ours! It would be March before No 87 finally sold, costing us more than quite a bit with the RBS. Maybe it was meant to be for there was SO much needing doing to the property.

The Caiystane scheme was built during the 1930s. What with the No 11 Tram terminating just up past the Braid Hills Hotel, car ownership was a must. It was obvious that these Bungalows were targeted at people of decent income. As a result, they all came with garages attached. Ours was no different, having one of the five 15amp power points provided! This was going to be a project on a big scale.

Arranging to have gas central heating installed required an upgrade in the supply across the garden – cooker only prior to that. A man hatch was required in each room floor for the pipework. This enabled Erik to go ahead with installing a ring mains electrical circuit. He went through two boilersuits scrabbling about in the approximately 18-inch void under the floorboards!

Decoration was my territory, and what a task. Our previous owner, a retired, widowed Master Butcher, had been a heavy smoker with the attendant staining throughout. The plus side was the beautiful hand-painted fireplace tiles. Inspection of those proved that not one single tile matched another. The front parlour/diner grate was also encased in a lovely Art Deco wood surrounded by polished oak. The little grates in the three bedrooms were also Deco with sunbursts above the fire opening. The fire in the back living room was a Baxi monstrosity, recesses in its hideous brickwork containing illuminated religious icons! That soon went, a multi-fuel stove replacing it—so cosy in the winter.

I was rather upset at the huge floor traps, but Hubby was thankful for them. Our floor-ripping plumber after a week said, "I'll see you again in a week's time." Enquiring just what was so important, our not being advised of such an event, he replied proudly, "I'll be speaking at the Earl's Court rally of Jehovah's Witnesses!" Meantime, I spent lots of my time at the top of Step ladders (the ceilings were high), scraping, sanding and painting. More especially when Hubby was on back shift, with the Hi-fi blaring MOBY to give me inspiration. Pricing a kitchen, it became apparent that we were now living in an area with a premium on any job quoted. So, Erik got stuck in and did it himself. He grumply called it the Caiystane Mark-up.

These properties were quite bespoke, buyers choosing different features to suit, but all behind the standard red and stone frontage. Our strange feature was the Panoramic Sash and Case windows in the back living room. Bad enough is the operation of the type, but really? The expansive windows, wider than they were tall, rendered their opening and closing almost impossible. French windows or Bi-fold doors might replace these oddities, but for reasons of space, we opted for sliding doors. The fitters of the same said they were the biggest home sliders they had fitted the width dictated by the old 'Panoramas.'

It was no quick job, taking more than a few months to transform the stained, dingy, quite depressing house—into a bright and airy lovely home. It's said that dreams don't just happen, they have to be worked at. We certainly did at No 9 Caiystane Avenue—and it was all worth it, to realise MY dream.

Tegan's 2005 birthday in June was our excuse to leave behind the DIY, and enjoy the company of Darren's family on the South Coast. Just a weekend break, however, as we had been advised that they planned a Scottish holiday in August.

So Erik and I cracked on with getting the two smaller bedrooms ready for their stay. When they did come, the weather was especially fine, so off we travelled together. Beach visits, street performers at the festival in the old town, the butterfly farm (the girls were spellbound at Auntie Erika handling a tarantula!), but the highlight was a visit to Alnwick Castle—the Harry Potter Magic School. In the rush of the pre-visit preparations, a hurried buy was a simple Ikea bed for Mia. She adored it! Never had a problem getting her to retire. All in all, I think they really enjoyed their vacation north of the border.

In October, due to lack of funds, it was a staycation (as it is now known) touring in the car. We based ourselves at the Banff Springs Hotel in the 'Brough,' enabling us to explore the area, also Moray. Hubby just had to visit the phone box in Pennan, the one featured in that wonderful film local hero. We still play the soundtrack album. An early December trip down to 10 QMR laden with Christmas Pressies brought the year to a close.

Time was now seeming to rush by but with nothing of import to record. That is until June 2006 when things turned very eventful. Darren's family came north to Edinburgh again coinciding with Tegan's birthday. Erika organised a table at Chiquito's Mexican Restaurant at Kinnaird Park for the occasion. She had previously been employed there, so some of the staff proved extra efficient at serving, also making a performance of the cake presentation. The most enjoyable party for all especially Tegan, of course.

At this time, I have to confess that Erika and I became quite conspiratorial in regard to Hubby's next-day celebration. He'd always resisted any fuss regarding the passing of his years, but there were now six decades of his life to mark. So, come the day, he was fussing about setting up for running a Barbie at No 9. Erika's exhortations for her father to smarten up were met with puzzlement, but she said she wasn't cracking the champagne with anyone in jeans. Reluctantly, he acceded, and the cork was popped, glasses raised.

Bubbly duly quaffed, the birthday boy was instructed to forget the BBQ and get in the car. Down to Slateford, we drove, to that delightful Chinese restaurant 'I Ching' (now no more), with Hubby beginning to warm to the idea of someone else doing the cooking. He became even more pleased when we entered for a private function, to be met by many surprise guests. As well as most of my family and Darren's, his old Pal Willie Binns was there to wish him the best, as were his brother Victor and wife Elaine—the Trio travelling down from Shetland. Much further travelled, however, was his big sister Peggy all the way from Edmonton, Canada.

Not often lost for words is my hubby, but I think flabbergasted sums him up—at least till the food was served. A great time for all. As things wound down, I thought, time to relax soon. No such luck, the birthday boy invited everyone back to No 9! The evening was spent, thanks to a particularly balmy night, outdoors on the patio and back garden. Erik would not be forgetting his 60th, that's for sure.

I didn't get much rest even after that as the next day we saw off Darren's family. Now beds to change, laundry washing to do, and still an evening meal to prepare. This I served in our front parlour to guests Willie, Vic, Elaine, Peggy and of course Erika (who assisted). While Peggy remained at Erika's flat we, whenever possible took car trips with her.

Otherwise, we advised her to purchase a Lothian Bus Day-Saver, and she did her own thing.

Hardly time to take a breath, it was off up to Shetland, this time to a Hamefarin. Erik's first cousin Iain McAlpine's eldest son had married in Johannesburg, South Africa (their hometown), and had travelled with his bride and Shetland parents for a second reception. This was held at the Whiteness Village Hall, and a great night was had by: all. For us, it was again the length of Britain travelled as come August, we winged it to the shores of the English Channel. A warm welcome, as always, awaited us at 10 QMR.

Still no Continental holidays, but instead in September, we set off north to 'do' the top of Scotland by car. Hotel Deals and BnBs were our night-time stop-overs, but daytime saw many miles covered—mostly in glorious weather. At times it was unwise to leave the car for photos, as you soon had unwelcome company—the Midge!

Another Pressie-carrying trip to Portchester to see my lovely grandgirls in early December was followed by a gorgeous Christmas Dinner at Erika's flat, to round off the year.

January and May 2007 saw us breaking up the monotony of work with hotel deals over weekends. Firstly, it was a short drive to Stirling, to a central hotel formed from a former school. A magnificent building up the hill towards the castle. Dining was enjoyed in the Refectory! We found it really handy for strolling and shopping. Secondly, we headed south and west to Dumfries and the Aston Hotel at the Crichton. Recently refurbished, it was very pleasant. Exploring the area was interesting and most enjoyable – forgotten Scotland.

Usually bypassed by Scots heading south, but appreciated by the Northern English!

On the home front, things were not so good. It looked like my dream home was under threat. My first cousin Joan who, as previously mentioned, was re-connecting with her Scottish relatives, had told me in confidence that cancer was upon her. We had, through visits to my uncle and aunt, established contact with her many years back, and with their passing still took time to visit her at Riding Mill. On one such trip, she confided her wish to leave me £25,000. I was shaken, but she was firm in her resolve, saying that I was the sister she might have had and grown up with.

Well, sadly, she had passed away in December 2005. In Midsummer, 2006, upon probate, I was informed that I was bequeathed only £5,000. Glad I was to receive anything in her memory, but upon enquiring with her solicitors, it transpired that a Codicil had been made just three weeks prior to her passing. Her £1,000 bequest to a Religious Order had increased 32×fold!

Erik said it was a common practice, however dubious, and when it comes to money some people act like 'Craas roon a Crang' (Crows round a carcase). Common or not, it left us in a bit of a fix, as I had set my sights on the figure covering improvements at No 9. Our interest payments were substantial, so it was with great reluctance that we decided to sell.

In the midst of all this, a situation arose that caused me no small measure of heartache. Becoming power of attorney for my stepdad, a sister had sight of documentation to the effect that a brother had, years back, entered into 'Right to Buy' with his mother and father. Doubtful indeed, that she might have any knowledge of any such deal, and given her fragile mental state, my mother was unlikely to have signed a will pursuant to her share of the property. A draft copy of such a document was shown to me, and where, should she be pre-deceased by her husband, her percentage share would pass with her 'love, favour and affection' to her four children! To say I was dumbfounded was no exaggeration. So, yet another night of sleep deprivation—wondering, questioning. To think that if my mother hadn't entered into her marriage, to secure a roof over my head, none of my siblings would exist. Now, apparently, it was me who didn't exist!

Chapter 20

Happy times for us come August 2007 in that the grandgirls flew up in the company of Auntie Erika, to Edinburgh for their holidays. With Darren at sea and Jane unable to get leave to fit in with the schools, the girls weren't going to miss out on a Scottish break. Lots of days out, including Tegan's favourite the Sea Pond at North Berwick. They were spellbound, however, in the museum watching the Millenium Clock in operation.

We did hook up with Darren at the month's end, as his research ship was docking near Largs for a few days. So, with Erika in tow, it was off to Largs for a restaurant rendezvous, followed by a pub visit. His work on board the James Cook took him all over the globe. He had worked his way up to become a technician in charge—team leader, as they say nowadays. He was amazed after one trip to find that HR had decided to rename all posts, and he would henceforth carry the title 'Cruise Director!'

While waiting for all the legalities to fall into place regarding selling and buying property, we took a nice weekend stay in Belfast. The city was still rebuilding tourism, and its confidence, after all the 'Troubles.' A coach tour of Antrim meant witnessing the geological marvel that is the

Giant's Causeway. A What's On guide told us of a performance by a Brass Band at the Botanic Gardens, on Sunday. So, grabbing some Sannies and small bottles of red wine, we made our way there. The Botanics are, of course, not a patch on the Inverleith premises, but we soon found ourselves at the Bandstand, We were welcomed by the bandmaster, who went on to say that the performance would unfortunately be curtailed. This, due to the Parkie seeing fit to not set up the folding chairs for the musicians. More especially though in respect of their Tuba player! It didn't put a damper on their playing, mostly brass standards and marches, but we were all 'blown' away with the finale—a rousing Temple of Doom.

The month of October saw us Flit from our lovely Caiystane Bungalow, just down the road to No.57 Howe Park. A much smaller detached Bungalow with an odd, long narrow lounge. Besides a regular bathroom, the smaller of the two bedrooms had an annexe attached containing a WC and wash hand basin.

We felt the property was ripe for expansion, and had plans prepared and applied for. These being granted, we soon had building firms knocking at the door. The layout was radically altered, and along with a not huge extension to the front, it would become a much more pleasant living space. Hubby needed a garage, what with his two classics and commuter bike. Our chosen builder agreed that it was the first priority—ideal for safe storage throughout the build for tools and materials.

Prior to any garage building and soon after moving in, Erik purchased a large shed to store his classics. Looking to the future he had ordered a longer roof for same. Once the

Bikes moved into the newly built garage, he bracketed the overhang, swapped the double doors for glazed units and lined out the interior, thereby creating a little Summerhouse. Many an evening we would take tea with the late afternoon sun warming our little hideaway. On Saturday afternoons especially, listening to Lisa Tarbuck on Hubby's old valve radio that I had bought for his birthday a few years back—it was a tall Ferranti.

Near neighbours had a toddler named Max, who delighted in Erik's bike noise, apparently announcing upon hearing it, 'Eyick! Eyick!' Strangely, whenever Hubby operated the Fly-Mo, he would burst into tears at the din!

Early December and it was our usual Pressie-carrying trip to Queen Mary Road, and catch up with Darren's family. Festive fare, due to our home circumstances, was provided at Christmas and New Year at Forrester Park—Erika's tasty cooking always appreciated.

2008 saw Hubby and I flying south to the Canaries for the first time. Gran Canaria in fact. Our resort was in Maspalomas with its huge spread of sandy beaches, all the way back to Playa del Ingles. Apparently, that incredible resort was named after an elderly English gentleman who, in the 1950s, chose to live hermit style on the barren shore— mostly devoid of any clothing! Many hundreds of holidaymakers can be encountered on the sands today, similarly (un) dressed.

West of the beach and beyond the Pharo (Lighthouse), are huge hotels and an esplanade of boutiques, restaurants, and jewellery emporiums. A wonderful way to round off each day was strolling the strip, eating and drinking as you go, with the sun sinking below the horizon. Needless to say, we were quite taken with the resort.

Mia's birthday beckoned come February, so it was off down to Hampshire again to visit Darren and his family—and join in the celebration. Thenceforth, along with my steady work at 'Carol's,' our trips away were for the most part spent in Portchester, and occasionally returning to Gran Canaria for a Vitamin D top-up! with Darren's family usually up to Edinburgh at least once a year, it was always lovely to see them all.

A significant event in January 2009 was our Ruby anniversary, 40 years! This we celebrated at the Dalmahoy Hotel with the family and friends. Hubby presented me with a gorgeous Ruby and Diamond ring. Also celebrating their 40th that year were Erik's first cousin Iain and his wife Mona, who travelled all the way from their home in South Africa to Shetland. A June trip up to Hubby's homeland was on the cards, and a great time we had, both at the reception and dance, but also catching up with friends and relations there.

Quite a year so far, and it wasn't over by a long chalk. October 18th arrived with the realisation that I no longer had to work! My birth year made me eligible for a pension at age 60 and I took full advantage. A lovely birthday celebration was arranged by Erika in the Norton House Hotel - again with family and friends attending.

It was now time, I had decided, to indulge myself at the closure of my business. The car that I adored, my Volvo V70, was increasingly showing signs that a major expense was looming in regard to its engine. With the UK government scrappage scheme in place, now might be the time to have my very first new car! An order was placed with Volvo at Sighthill, and I looked forward to a car bespoke to my wishes. The V70 was T5 engined, similar to those of the Constabulary

—a wolf in sheep's clothing. I would delight when some young Spiv would pull up alongside me in a big BMW, or the like. A disdainful look was all it took for me to floor the pedal on the green light and leave it in my wake!

We left the car at the showroom as requested for scrappage certification and processing, and returned home to await a phone call for my new V50. The V70 was becoming a memory as we bussed it out a few days later to pick up my 'Gleaming wheels!' we were introduced to the car by an effusive salesman, and not wishing any upset, I let Hubby drive me home—I would familiarise myself on quieter roads later. Off we set, turned one corner, and there being loaded on the transporter for scrapping and crushing, was my V70. Tears? Oh, yes!

A November Tyne-side trip in the car was our first longish outing, and delighted I was – I do love the smell of new leather! A few weeks later, we couldn't use the car, there was snow at Howe Park—knee-deep!

When 2010 arrived, and with my settling into retirement mode, I resolved to investigate that which had, at times, given me many nights of difficulty sleeping. I would lie abed thinking, perhaps too much, of events in my past many un-explained.

Who was my real father?

Did I have sisters and brothers, other than those I grew up with?

If I'd been adopted, would I have known my own mother as an aunt?

Why did I carry the name of my stepdad, when in fact he never adopted me at all? My marriage certificate revelation that I had my mum's name Mackenzie might have spared me the indignity of being cat-called at school as 'Stinky Farter!' Just like the blink of grandad in Inverness all those years ago, one day on the top deck of the No 10 bus, Mum said, "There's your real father." Not a blink of him did I get, as the bus rolled along.

What did he look like?

Was he dark-haired like me?

Did he become swarthy with sunshine like me?

It was time to find out.

Back in my Shetland years, a client told me of how she, being only fifteen, was taken to Aberdeen to give birth. The baby was immediately removed for adoption, and she was told to forget all about it. Easy for some to say. Many years later, she said she approached the organisation Birthlink to find her little boy—and they met. I now thought it was perhaps time that I should contact Birthlink.

Not with any great expectation, in August of the year, I made enquiries with the local branch in Edinburgh. Less than two months later, an immense of paperwork came my way. Freedom of Information granted access to all records of my time at St Katherine's Children's Home. Also, social work records gave up my mum's story and the circumstances leading to my arrival, plus her tribulations thereafter. It all made for interesting reading, explaining many things, but nothing regarding my actual father. It would be eight long months before I once more heard from Birthlink.

But, come up with the goods they did. With only his name as Mum knew it, Richie Richardson, and that he was a joiner in the building trade, their exhaustive search brought up quite a few of that surname. However, not one Richard Richardson did they find. Many and varied were the occupations of the candidates, and it looked as though my hopeful search would be in vain. The closest to Mum's putative assertion of his name, and a joiner, was a certain Laurence Richardson. More enquiries, at a more personal level by Birthlink, established that Laurence had, since infant school, carried the moniker, Richie. Bingo!

A tentative enquiry with the eldest Son of Richie's—Edward, held these facts as positive. When asked if, on my behalf, that contact might be made with the extended family, he declined. His widowed mother was still alive, and he did not wish to visit any upset on her, or her family. I was, of course, rather disappointed at this point, but then neither would I wish any upset to anyone. I was provided with a photo of Richie, at work in his carpenter's apron, constructing I know not what. He was undoubtedly dark of hair, but being a black and white pic, that's all I could glean from it.

It would appear that Richie was a serial philanderer, and had cheated on Edward's mum. Not only that, he went on to have another family with wife no 2—who he also cheated on! Edward had little good to say of his father. Weirdly, it turned out that our over-the-hedge neighbour at Currie, who I always thought looked a bit like me, was in fact Edward—who saved Hubby's motorbikes in our garage fire!

40th Anniversary (Photo: Darren Young)

My one and only new car (Photo: Erik Young)

On Reflection

I do still to this day; wish I had asked more questions. However, readers will have gathered that my situation in childhood was less than conducive for introspection, far less interrogation of my parents. It was always my attitude that whatever the situation or circumstance, one should strive to surmount those same situations and circumstances. I learned early that nothing was going to fall in my lap, and only through hard work and application would I realise what I hoped for. Much as I would have loved ten children, expediency ruled against it. I regard myself as blessed with my daughter Erika and son Darren, my two grandgirls, Tegan and Mia.

With me, throughout all life's ups and downs, I have a Hubby who's still in the frame! He, who as a bit of a poet, would at some point in our time together, jot down these words…

> *So I bless each day that comes my way,*
> *that she truly is my wife.*
> *And every day I'm truly glad,*
> *that she would want me in her life.*

Acknowledgments

Sincere thanks are due to one of my earliest clients, Val Bewick, for her encouragement—and for my only start-up gift: £20.

Gratitude also goes to Hay and Co., who, on more than one occasion, showed great patience regarding monies owed for our two building projects. Every penny was paid as I earned it. Perhaps having Nancy and Kay Garriock as clients helped with that!

A special thanks to Willie Reid, the Royal Bank agent who arranged a loan for equipment and stock—thanks in part to the kind recommendation of his wife, who had faith in my skills.

To our Edinburgh joiner and his assistant, Erik: a massive thank you for your tireless work on the 5/7 conversion and the building of Clossbiggin.

And last, but by no means least, heartfelt thanks to Hubby, for patiently transcribing my words—first in longhand, then with his trusty one-finger typing!

Notes

Ch.6.
Our first home, in Leith, was at 13 Graham Street. Our Close entry faced the top of West Bowling Street.

Ch.9.
Our Nesting to Lerwick move was to 29 Norstane.

Ch.11.
Our first Jugoslavian holiday was in 1982.
Earl-sized refers to Shetland's little inter-island steamer, prior to the introduction of Ro-Ro car ferries.

Ch.12.
Sai Chun Ma was the owner, and initially, manager of the Golden Coach. When his family moved to Edinburgh, he remained as proprietor, but with family managing. Now running a restaurant in Morrison Street opposite the cinema, he one day collapsed at home and tragically died instantly. His passing reverberated throughout the Isles.

Ch.13.
Fiddle Box Carriers are two young lads (12+ years) who assist a Guizing squad throughout the long night. More than fiddle boxes are carried, however, usually 'heads' and other bits of equipment for the sketch performed in each venue.

Ch.14.
Charlie Summers was, like Sonny, a janitor but at Anderson High School, not the Central School.
Bressay Ward is a prominent conical hill on the island that forms Bressay Sound-Lerwick's harbour.

Ch.18.
Peerie is the Shetland dialect for small/little.

Ch.20.
Yet one more hindrance to air travel, post 9/11, was the withdrawal of the UM service. This was whereby children of a suitable age could travel minus parental care. A flight attendant would meet up with Unaccompanied Minors (UMs) at the check-in desk. From there, they looked after said children until arrival at their destination, where they handed their charges over.

Ch.20.
Erika flew down to accompany the girls at Darren's expense. On the kids' return with her, she stayed on for a break with his family in Portchester. In the dear dead days of BEA/BA domestic flights, and with a friendly pilot, a child might even fly in the 'Jump' seat up in the cockpit!